D1255031

A MAGNIFICENT FARCE

AND

OTHER DIVERSIONS OF A
BOOK-COLLECTOR

" URIZEN "

From an original water-color drawing by William Blake, in his most Michael-Angelesque style

A MAGNIFICENT FARCE

AND OTHER DIVERSIONS
OF A BOOK-COLLECTOR

BY

ALFRED EDWARD NEWTON, *1864 - 1940*

WITH ILLUSTRATIONS

Essay Index Reprint Series

 BOOKS FOR LIBRARIES PRESS
FREEPORT, NEW YORK

First Published 1921
Reprinted 1970

INTERNATIONAL STANDARD BOOK NUMBER:
0-8369-1767-7

LIBRARY OF CONGRESS CATALOG CARD NUMBER:
73-121492

PRINTED IN THE UNITED STATES OF AMERICA

TO
WILLIAM MAXWELL SCOTT

*For over twenty-five years we have been
yoked to the same plough, and if we have
kept the furrow straight, it is because we
have pulled together.*

PURELY PERSONAL

BY WAY OF INTRODUCTION

It was inevitable, after the success of "The Amenities of Book-Collecting," that its author should attempt to repeat that success, and — You, kind or, it may be, suspicious reader, shall fill up that blank. Whatever your verdict may be, I shall accept it unhesitatingly; for one never knows, one's self, whether a piece of work, or sundry pieces, upon which one has been engaged for a long time, have merit or not. Our little quips and quiddities, once spontaneous, after having been written in pencil on odd scraps of paper, and typed by one's secretary in her leisure moments, look rather feeble when the galley proof comes in, and positively silly on the printed page. This is a risk we who print books must run. Nothing venture, nothing have.

Long ago, before years and tobacco had destroyed a voice naturally defective, I was singing cockney songs, to my own delight but to the qualified enjoyment of my audience, when someone turning to me remarked: "Why, I had no idea that you sang!" To which Felix Schelling, not then enjoying an international reputation as a scholar, rejoined slyly: "I am not sure that he does." And so it may prove to be with my writing. I have never been able to free my mind of the truth of that remark of Gray's: "Any fool may write a valuable book by chance, if he will only tell us what he heard and saw, with veracity." Trollope is said to have damaged his reputation by his confession as to the way in which he wrote; at the risk of utterly destroying mine, I want to say that any style I may have acquired is the result of writing advertisements of electrical apparatus for many years. When one is selling a page of writing, one receives, I suppose, as much as five, or even twenty-five dollars a page. When one is buying a page of advertising, one pays anywhere from one hundred to five thousand dollars a page! The discriminating reader will discover upon which page the most time is spent. Those who write with ease, to show their breeding, forget the last line of the couplet,— usually attributed to Byron, that "easy writing's damned hard reading."

When one is the victim of a practical joke, one tries to forget it; so, when several universities tagged me and gave me the legal right to append certain letters to my name, I said to myself: "Here is a fine opportunity for you to make a fool of yourself; disappoint your friends by not embracing it." And so it is that I was soon able to break my friends of the habit of giving me a title, all except a certain head waiter and my barber, who seemed to feel that the size of their tips depended upon the loudness or frequency with which they called me "Doctor."

Only yesterday it happened that, while I was sitting in the reading-room of my club, a page entered and called out, "Dr. Newton!" I went on with my newspaper, and he spoke again: "Dr. A. Edward

Newton!" He would be denied no longer, and, looking at him guiltily, I was told I was wanted on the telephone. Crossing the room, I experienced sundry difficulties. I thought I knew who was calling me — my friend Hawley McLanahan, the architect, the merits of whose Scotch make one reluctant to break with him; but this must be stopped at any cost. Entering the telephone booth, I took up the receiver, and without any preliminaries I requested him to go to the devil, and promptly.

Reader! have you ever heard a lady go into an apoplexy? Well, that is the sound I heard from the other end of the wire. Of course I administered what relief I could, and prostrated myself before her — a difficult thing to do in a telephone booth; and finally, she being somewhat restored, I asked to what I owed the pleasure of this call.

"Why," replied the lady, "I hoped you would consent to make a few remarks at a 'Current Events' luncheon we are having for the benefit of the starving in China. Christopher Morley had promised to come, but he has met with an accident." [1]

"Why don't you get Tom Daly?" I inquired; "he's worth a dozen of us."

"He's in New England lecturing," was the reply.

"I see," I said, "I'm the last chance. I can't possibly tell a lady to go to the devil a second time. I'll come; and your Current Eventers will wish that they were starving with the Chinese."

And so it proved.

[1] Mr. Morley wishes it known that his hoof is broken, not cloven.

May I relate how the "Amenities" restored to me a long-lost sweetheart? It came about in this way. I received one day in my mail a letter from a lady, thus conceived : —

DEAR SIR, — I am wondering whether "The Amenities of Book-Collecting and Kindred Affections" would preclude the exchange of our handiwork! If not, I should be glad to forward copies of "The Four Horsemen of the Apocalypse" and "Mare Nostrum" in exchange for the "Amenities of Book-Collecting," some chapters of which I greatly enjoyed when they appeared in the "Atlantic Monthly." With kind regards to those of your family who remember me, I am, very sincerely your old-time Rahway [N.J.] neighbor on the other side of the fence,

CHARLOTTE BREWSTER JORDAN.

Of course, Lottie Brewster! We had known each other intimately as children ; how stupid of me not to have remembered, when I had been reading everywhere of her translation of a novel selling as no novel has ever sold before.

I despatched the "Amenities" forthwith, saying that I was receiving far more than I gave,— which, indeed, was the case, for the inscriptions put the volumes high in the "association" class,— and upon my next visit to New York I called on my old-time friend and we had a delightful hour together. In the course of our chat over old times, I said : "Lottie, perhaps you can tell me what has become of my friend Jennie

M——. She was my first love. I remember our fond parting when, as a boy of thirteen, I went away to school. I remember, too, returning, still a boy, to find my sweetheart a young woman, with dresses much longer than those young women are wearing nowadays, and quite indifferent to me. I tried to awaken in her some spark of the old sentiment, but failed and knew that my heart was broken."

"Why," said Lottie, "Jennie is living in New York. I see her occasionally. She is rich, good-looking, and a widow. I am sure she would be glad to see you."

"I know nothing about that," I said; "but I am coming to New York very soon, to make an address at the Grolier Club on William Blake. It is a meeting of woman artists or woman sculptors, or something. There will be tea afterwards and cake; indeed, that will be the most enjoyable part of the affair. I shall be the only man, and for ten minutes a hero. I want Jennie to witness my triumph."

So it was arranged, and a few weeks later the party came off.

While I was reading my paper, I observed just in front of me a demure little lady, exquisitely gowned, her hair rather more than touched with gray; and at the end of my address I went forward.

"Jennie," I said, putting my arm around her.

"O Eddie, stop!" she cried, just as she did at parting more than forty years before.

Like causes still produce like effects. Invitations and counter-invitations followed in quick succession; and Carolyn Wells, hearing of what was going on, signaled, "Wait a minute till I change my frock; I'm from Rahway, too."

And Carolyn Wells's presence resulted in such goings-on that I began to wonder whether the by-product of authorship was not the best part of it.

And out of the shadow of the years long past rose Van Antwerp, formerly Willie, also of Rahway, my oldest friend, who, almost fifty years ago, was always to be found playing in my back-yard when I was not playing in his. Tired of beating and being beaten up in Wall Street, he had retired with the substantial fragments of several fortunes, to spend his declining years (and may they be many) in content — and California, to which he invited me.

In the midst of the renewal of old associations and the making of a host of new acquaintances, I discovered that I was not in very robust health. This is not my own discovery. I paid a physician a handsome fee for making it. His advice was: "Go slow. You have been pelting along for forty years; it's time to relax. Let someone else do your work. You have a hearty son in business — let him work; and your partner. He impressed me as a very forceful fellow; he will probably be glad to have his own way a little more than he can when you are around. Give him his head. It is a great mistake you business men make of thinking that no one can take your place. I have no doubt that there are half a dozen men in your office who can do your work better than you do. How about smoking," he continued; "how many cigars?"

To this I replied: "Doctor, there are some things too sacred for words, there are some things that men do not tell even their wives; but, in point of fact, I have always smoked in moderation, never more than one cigar at a time; three after breakfast, four after lunch —"

"That will do; that accounts for much. We will omit the cigars after breakfast entirely, and hereafter your limit will be one after lunch and one after dinner; on holidays, birthdays, and the like, you may smoke two after dinner — mild ones. No more excesses of any kind. Do not run for trains, and do not climb steps unnecessarily. What exercise do you take?"

"Very little," I replied, "I am of Joe Chamberlain's opinion that to walk downstairs in the morning and upstairs at night is enough exercise for any gentleman."

"A little extreme," said my physician, "but not bad advice for you; and when you sit, keep your feet up."

"On the mantelpiece?" I inquired.

"I said no excesses," replied the physician; "the table will do. Lessen the pull on your heart-muscle. Do not play more than nine holes of golf on a flat course."

"How about the nineteenth hole?" I said.

"Well," said he, "with whiskey at twenty dollars a bottle, you will not be likely to play that hole to excess. You do not look as if you ever had. Don't worry, avoid excitement, and keep your mind occupied. Take up reading. Did n't someone tell me that you had written a book? Write another one, a long one, and then go to Europe, where the criticisms of it will not annoy you. My prophecy is that you will live to be a disagreeable old man. Take these pills three times a day, and come to see me in a month. Good-morning."

And as I exited, another victim entered, and was received with the same sympathetic interest.

"This is just what the doctor ordered," I said, as I rolled away from his door in my motor. I sat back, put my feet up, and tried to feel a superannuated man, and made a failure of it. "Let someone else do your work!" What music was in these words! "Write a book!" What fun! "Go to Europe!" more fun! I always said I was lucky, and for once my friends agree with me.

I'm off!

A. EDWARD NEWTON.

DAYLESFORD HOUSE
422 SOUTH CARLISLE STREET
PHILADELPHIA, *May* 15, 1921

CONTENTS

ILLUSTRATIONS

ILLUSTRATIONS

A MAGNIFICENT FARCE

AND

OTHER DIVERSIONS OF A BOOK-COLLECTOR

A MAGNIFICENT FARCE

I

A MAGNIFICENT FARCE

In the good old days at the theatre, say a hundred years or so ago, it was not unusual for the main feature of the evening's entertainment to be preceded by a little curtain-raiser; in like manner, the farce to which I am going to ask your attention is to be preceded by a necessarily brief résumé of perhaps the greatest burlesque ever written.

I refer to the trial of Mr. Pickwick, the immortal creation of a young and practically unknown man, who for a time masqueraded under the pseudonym of Boz. (Pronounced not as we usually pronounce it, but as if there were an *e* at the end of it; it was a corruption of Mose.)

Mr. Pickwick, who is as English as Falstaff, and I think as great a creation, had inquired his landlady's opinion as to the greater expense involved in keeping two people rather than one, having in mind engaging not himself, but a man, Sam Weller, to look after him, as the phrase goes. Forthwith, the landlady, Mrs. Bardell, assumes that Mr. Pickwick has made her an offer of marriage, flings her arms about his neck, and at his appeal to "consider — if anyone should come," cries, "Let them come."

And come they did : young Master Bardell and Mr. Tupman, Mr. Winkle, and Mr. Snodgrass. The astonishment of all was extreme. His friends did not at the time know him for the amiable gentleman he subsequently became, and regarded his astonishing behavior with some suspicion.

How Mrs. Bardell, through that precious pair of legal practitioners,— Messrs. Dodson and Fogg,— brought action against Mr. Pickwick for breach of promise of marriage, with damages laid at £1500 ; how his friends were made to testify against him ; how Sam Weller was promptly ordered to "stand down" when he began to tell how generous it was in those legal gentlemen to take the case "on spec," and to charge nothing at all for costs unless they got them out of Mr. Pickwick, is known even to Macaulay's schoolboy, if there ever was such a prodigy.

Had the elder Weller's advice been taken, an "alleybi" would have been provided — a strong "alleybi" has indeed solved many a legal problem ; but Mr. Pickwick would not hear of such a thing, and judgment was given for the plaintiff with damages at £750.

How Mr. Pickwick, declining to pay, is cast into the Fleet, and how Mrs. Bardell, having given a *cognovit*, whatever that may be, for the costs, also finds her way into the famous old prison ; their meeting, and how, by the payment of all the costs, Mr. Pickwick finally secures the release of the lady and himself and their escape from the legal toils of the two scamps, Dodson and Fogg — all this has been written for all the world to read. And all the world has read it. Mr. Pickwick is immortal, not only as a character, but also in the sense in which the word immortal is used by Chesterton, who points out that Mr. Pickwick was a fairy; not that he was suited to swing on a trapeze of gossamer; but that if, while so swinging, he had fallen upon his head, his pains would not have been severe, and he would not have died.

I take it that the so-called trial of Mr. Pickwick is known to more people the world over than any other scene in any book whatever (the Bible excepted). Call it what you will,— comedy, high or low, or farce, or burlesque,— it remains the most famous picture of an innocent man temporarily deprived of his liberty and the pursuit of happiness, which after all was Mr. Pickwick's serious business. There is one other trial which, in some respects, resembles it, and that is the trial of Warren Hastings. Both trials were farces; one was mean and sordid, the other was magnificent. In one, a conviction was secured; in the other, an acquittal. But in both cases the result was the same — the victims paid the costs.

My home happens to be at Daylesford, on the "Main Line" of the Pennsylvania Railroad; and while the "Main Line" means little to those who are not of the Quaker City, those who are know that it is — Spruce Street — emancipated somewhat. Many of the stations have pretty names — Welsh for the most part; for the district was taken up by Welsh settlers a century or two ago — and Daylesford is not the least pretty. It is hardly in the Welsh tract, and gets its name rather curiously from the English home of Warren Hastings; for the reason that he was the hero of an old man who once lived in these parts, and who was given the privilege of naming the little shed and platform which have served for a station since the railroad people concluded that a stop at this particular point might be advisable.

One distinction Daylesford has, in common with a number of other hamlets and villages hereabouts: it is only a few miles from Valley Forge, where the soldiers of the Revolutionary army under Washington, when its fortunes were at the lowest, spent the terrible winter of 1777–78. It is also within rifle-shot of the fine old colonial mansion where Anthony Wayne was born,— Mad Anthony,— subsequently commander-in-chief of the army, as a bronze tablet let into its south wall very properly records. Hence we all are supposed to be somewhat conversant with colonial affairs.

One evening, as I was going out on my usual train, a large, pompous man, whom I knew slightly, condescendingly lowered himself into the seat beside me, remarking as he did so: "I see you frequently on this train. Where do you live? You go farther up the line than I do."

I told him the name of my station, which, being a very insignificant one, he had never heard of; and then, probably to keep me from reading my newspaper, he observed: "Daylesford. It's a pretty

name. Gets its name from a ford in a dale, I suppose."

"No," I replied, "there is no ford there." Then
I told him of Daylesford in England having been the
home of Warren Hastings, and that our little station
had been named in his honor, and how I had often
thought it a rather curious matter altogether; when,
to my surprise, my friend seemed inclined to take
exception to my attitude, and remarked: "Not at all;
I think it fine, the way we keep alive the names of
those old Revolutionary heroes. We don't do enough
of it. There ought to be a monument to him at Valley Forge."

Fortunately my astonishment was covered by the
conductor throwing open the car door and announc-
ing "Bryn Mawr!" Whereupon my companion
bade me good-evening, and left me to my meditations.

After dinner, lighting a ´cigar, I strolled about my
library, murmuring to myself, "The Hall was worthy
of the trial; it had resounded with acclamations at
the coronations of thirty kings," — or some such
matter. I had not read Macaulay's essay on Warren
Hastings, which is one of his best, for many years;
but these purple patches have a way of fixing themselves, somewhat unsteadily perhaps, even in so poor
a memory as mine. The subject haunted me, but I
could not remember whether the great trial had resulted in a conviction or an acquittal, or exactly what
it was about. "High crimes and misdemeanors" —
my memory seemed to say. It might not be a bad

idea to revive a faded recollection. I had expected to be through with Warren Hastings before I had finished my cigar, but a year was to elapse before I was tired of the subject. One of the joys of being a desultory reader is that one may read as one chooses.

An immense amount has been written on Warren Hastings, but, as is usual, when Macaulay has written upon a subject, what he has said is remembered, and all else is forgotten. At this late day a phrase much employed by one of Hastings's biographers, "Be this as it may," suggests that one can take one's choice of the many contradictory statements and draw one's own conclusions. Of a few facts we may be quite certain.

Warren Hastings was born in Oxfordshire, in 1732, of a very old family, then impoverished; his great-grandfather had disposed of the ancestral estate, Daylesford, and at the time of his birth the family was living in great poverty. For such education as he received, he was indebted to his uncle. At an early age he was sent as a "King's scholar" to Westminster School, where he did well. On the death of his uncle, a guardian secured for him a situation in the India Office, and shortly afterwards, at the age of eighteen, he sailed for Calcutta. There he prospered and married. His wife and several children dying, Hastings used his immense energies and ability in the service of his country, incidentally increasing his fortune. After fourteen years' residence, he returned to England, pensioned his uncle's widow, and otherwise providing for his family, occupied his leisure with Oriental studies and society. His investments proving unfortunate, and his knowledge of Indian affairs being constantly sought, he was finally prevailed upon to go out to India a second time; and with his second journey to India his life may be said to have begun.

He was low in funds and in spirits when he set out; and on the voyage, which in those days was an affair of many months, he fell ill and was nursed back to health by a beautiful and accomplished Baroness von Imhoff, who was accompanying her husband to India, and with whom he fell in love. Imhoff, a German portrait-painter, proved complaisant, and finally accepted a proposition of Hastings to the effect that, in return for a substantial cash payment, he should permit the baroness to secure a divorce and become Mrs. Hastings. The legal formalities took years to arrange; meanwhile, nature took its course and the baron resided — where the baroness was not.

One may again refer to Macaulay's schoolboy as to the manner in which Hastings, as Governor-General, wrote his name upon Britain's empire in the East. It occupied him for sixteen years. His instructions were vague; they might perhaps be summed up in a sentence: "Remember that Indian affairs are primarily business affairs, and that dividends are expected; and, by the way, if you can extend the sweep of the Empire, it will be appreciated and perhaps outweigh the loss of the colonies in America, which have recently been giving us much trouble."

Hastings was far from home and self-reliant; to ask a question of the ministers of the Crown in London, and get a reply, was a matter of perhaps two years, by which time the crisis that had compelled the question was over. Hastings, on the ground, did what seemed to him best for all concerned. Moreover, he was not alone in the government. There was a council of five over which he presided, which claimed to have the right of review of the acts of the Governor-General. Sir Philip Francis, now generally regarded as the author of the Junius Letters, was a member of the Council, and from the moment of his arrival in India became an enemy of Hastings. Originally the difficulty seems to have arisen over the absence of the ceremony with which Francis expected to be greeted. Misunderstandings and quarrels between them were frequent; finally the short and ugly word was used, and a duel fought. Francis was severely wounded, and although a reconciliation was attempted, it was not successful.

There was undoubtedly plenty of room for honest differences of opinion as to the wisdom, to say nothing of the legality, of many of Hastings's acts. He may have been cruel, as was subsequently charged, but his position was difficult in the extreme. He was sailing an uncharted sea, and he was serving his King and country rather than himself. Most men who served in India after a few years returned home rich. The word Nabob was coined for them; they were a national scandal at a time when public morality was low. According to the standards of his time, Has-

tings was unexceptionable in his conduct. To judge
him by the standards of another time is absurd;
rather we should remember the reply of his great contemporary Clive, when charged with having made,
by devious means, a great fortune: "When I think of
the possibilities of the case, I am surprised at my own
moderation." Only the Germans, and perhaps the
Irish, can doubt that England's rule in India has been
in the main beneficent. This is not to say that no
deeds were done which Englishmen should look back
upon with shame. *Be this as it may.*

Under a burning sun — as Napoleon said of the
battlefield — men soon grow old. Hastings finally
longed for home. He thought of England, and of
Daylesford, the estate of his ancestors, which he
would reacquire with a part of his fortune. As Governor of India he had accustomed himself to live in
regal splendor; he would continue so to live in England. His King, George III, having succeeded, practically unaided, in wrenching from his crown its most
valuable jewel, the American Colonies (acting upon
the advice of his mother, "George, be King!"), would
welcome with outstretched arms the man who had
added India to the British possessions. He would
receive a pension and a title; he would become Lord
Daylesford. He had no children, but he would hear
his wife, whom he loved devotedly, somewhat doting-
ly perhaps, addressed as "My Lady." Such was his
dream. When would his resignation be accepted?
At last relief came, and Hastings sailed for England.

The voyage home was unusually short. Hastings

sailed in February ; about the middle of the following
June he landed at Plymouth, and proceeded at once
to London, where his reception was all that he could
desire. He was received by the King, and, what was
quite as important, good Queen Charlotte received
Mrs. Hastings. Averse as she was known to be to
divorced persons, she appears to have looked upon
the Hastings's matrimonial escapade in India as due
either to the distance from civilization, or perchance
to the climate ; or perhaps she was moved by the gift
of a magnificent bedstead made entirely of carved
ivory, which Mrs. Hastings presented to her. *Be
this as it may*, the Hastings reception lacked nothing
in warmth, and all was going swimmingly, when
Edmund Burke rose in the House of Commons and
advised that he would at a future day make a motion
respecting the conduct of a gentleman just returned
from India ; and he was as good as his word. But it
required over two years properly to set the stage for
the great trial that was impending.

> What living mortal ever heard
> Any good of George the Third?

What malign fairy touched at birth that royal prince,
so that he became silly at his best, and at his worst
insane? But whatever may be the English feeling
for George III, it is not for us to complain of him.
Glorying, as he said he did, in being born a Briton,
he was in fact, as in family, a German, and of a bovine
intelligence especially fitting him to drive oxen. A
sequence of events gave, or appeared to give, him

a proud and liberty-loving people to drive, just at a time when English-speaking people were learning to drive themselves. To the end of his long life, his ill-success with them never ceased to amaze him. During the war,— now happily terminated with the elimination of all German princes, we may hope forever,— I heard an English army officer bring a large dinner-party to its feet by proposing "The health of the English-speaking peoples, once separated by a mad German king, now reunited by a mad German emperor." The effect was electrical.

But in 1785 George III, while by no means as sure of himself as when he came to the throne twenty-five years before, still felt that, if he chose to welcome warmly a man who appeared to have been more successful than himself in governing dependencies, he was at liberty to do so. But many and great changes had taken place in England during Hastings's absence — changes of which Hastings, who was an administrator rather than a politician, could know nothing, and which Majesty deemed unworthy of notice. The mere fact that Hastings was favorably received by the King raised up a party against him. The younger Pitt, who was in power, at once became suspicious. Hastings had probably forgotten his archenemy, Francis; but Francis had come to have great influence over Burke, then at the height of his reputation; and we are justified in believing that Burke was prompted, not alone by his partisan zeal, but by his love of justice, when he decided that Hastings's conduct in India should be reviewed in London.

The Indian question was then a difficult question, as the Irish question now is, and seemingly as impossible of solution. To say "India" was to start something. Instantly there was a division of public opinion. The King, the Court, and Lord Chancellor Thurlow all took Hastings's side. Burke ranged on his, Pitt, Sheridan, and Fox; indeed, almost without exception the most brilliant and forceful men in the nation. The preparation for the trial was the work of several years and the brief (?), when printed with its index, filled twenty-four folio volumes. Hastings wished to be defended by Erskine; but Erskine, while not afraid of Burke, admitted his inability to oppose Fox and Sheridan, and Hastings was obliged to content himself with a small group of relatively obscure men, led by one Edward Law, afterwards Lord Chief Justice Ellenborough, upon whom the burden of the defense chiefly rested. Heroic work was to be done. Hastings was appalled, as he had reason to be, by the scope and venom of the proceedings against him. He was alone and fighting a nation, not for his life but for his honor. There was no question of personal integrity. Out of the immense revenues which had passed through his hands, he appears to have saved for himself only £80,000 or so. If he could be convicted of wrongdoing, who had profited by it? England, the very England that seemed bent upon his destruction.

At last the time for the trial grew near. The great state trials of England have from time immemorial been held in Westminster Hall. No place of less dis-

CARD OF ADMISSION, SIGNED AND SEALED, TO THE TRIAL
OF WARREN HASTINGS

tinction was suited for so overwhelming a function. Society with a capital S began to pay attention. Heretofore the matter had been generally regarded as a squabble between factions; but it soon came to be understood that a magnificent entertainment was to be staged, the prosecuting committee being composed of nineteen men, who very properly became known as "the Managers." (The name was given them at the time, and it has passed into history.) Excitement could not have been more intense if a new vice had been discovered and was to be on exhibition. Society, which, in the picturesque phrase of Trevelyan, then floated from one amusement to another upon a sea of wine, set sail for Westminster. For the moment the clubs and gaming-tables were deserted.

It is early in the morning of the 13th of February, 1788. The approaches to the Hall are guarded by grenadiers; the streets are blocked by magnificent carriages of state; the demand for tickets is enormous, and fabulous prices are paid: as much as fifty pounds, it is said, is offered for a good location; and even to this day cards of admission, when duly signed and sealed, have a certain monetary value. The spectacle is to begin at eleven o'clock. Long before that hour, the Hall is packed: four hundred Lords and Commoners are in attendance. At last, the great functionaries of the trial begin to file into the grand old Hall, its gray walls concealed by crimson hangings. Two by two the representatives of the legal machinery of the nation enter: peers temporal and spiritual, judges and masters in Chancery, clerks and gentlemen-in-waiting. There are "Black Rod" and "Mace-Bearer," and the dukes of the Royal House, and, finally, that notorious scoundrel, the Prince of Wales himself, *alias* "The first Gentleman in Europe." The King is not present, being "indisposed" — this euphonious word concealing perhaps from a few the fact that Majesty is, for the time being, insane. The throne, therefore, is empty, but each person passing it makes a profound obeisance to it, and there is much talk as to who bows lowest or most gracefully.

About noon, all being in readiness, the Sergeant-at-arms cries: "Warren Hastings, come forth and save thee and thy bail." At once there appears a small and emaciated person, who, glancing around with evident anxiety, falls on his knees before the bar, but is at once told by the Lord Chancellor to rise. It is the formal procedure, but nothing is omitted that might tend to shake the confidence of the accused.

Thereupon the reading of the charges begins, and occupies two whole days; "rendered less tedious than it would otherwise have been by the silver voice and just emphasis of the clerk of the court," says Macaulay, who was not then born and hence was not obliged to sit through the proceedings; whereas Fanny Burney was, and gives it as her opinion that the reading was so monotonous that it was impossible to discover whether it was charge or answer.

"They're off!" is the cry for which we impatiently wait at the race-course, and thereafter all is confu-

sion. So it is at this trial. The throng, which has
held itself tense for hours, suddenly becomes relaxed.
From one part of the house to another, from one
box to another, stroll the wits and beaux of the day,
eyeing and ogling ladies who have come to be
eyed and ogled.

Sir Joshua Reynolds, who has lost or forgotten his
ear-trumpet, does not allow this mishap to interfere
with his usual good-humor, but smiles and bows to
everyone, the centre of a group of admiring friends.
Johnson's friend Wyndham saunters up to Miss
Burney, and congratulates her upon the location of
her seat. "Is it not a magnificent spectacle? You
see it here to great advantage; you lose some of the
Lords, but you gain all the ladies, ha! ha!"

"Yes, but what is going forward? I can't discover to which side I am listening."

"It's not important. They are only galloping
through the charges."

"Galloping through the charges? That's a form
of law, I suppose."

"Oh! look at the Archbishop of York affecting to
read the articles of impeachment! Spare your eyes,
my good Lord! we know that your mind is already
made up. Hastings has advanced your son's interest
in the East."

It was like a night at the opera, when the ballet is
on, and Society is more interested in itself than in
what takes place on the stage. We may be sure that
there was adjournment at the proper time for food,
and that tea was taken, and that the evening and the

morning were the first day, and the second was like
unto it. Finally, however, the Chancellor rose and
made a brief speech, and gave great offense to "the
managers" by the use of the word "mere." "Mere
allegations," he called the rhetoric inscribed upon the
immense rolls of parchment, the reading of which
had consumed two entire days — and these words
were to prove prophetic.

On the third day the trial really began. Burke as
Manager-in-chief rose and, making a profound bow
to the Court, stood forth as the accuser of Warren
Hastings, and in his opening address accused him of
every crime in the calendar. A famous judge, in
Polonius-manner, not long since summed up his advice to a young advocate in these words : "Above all,
avoid eloquence as you would the very devil"; but
in those days eloquence, or what passed for it, was
the delight of Lords and Commons alike, and Burke
was admittedly the greatest speaker of his time.

The man who did not know how to indict a whole
people had no difficulty whatever in indicting one
man of offenses enough to damn an entire nation.
He accused Hastings of all the crimes that have their
rise in the wicked dispositions of men — avarice,
rapacity, pride, cruelty, malignity of temper, haughti-
ness, insolence; in short, everything that manifests a
heart blackened and gangrened to the core. With
this as an introduction, he proceeded to charge him
with having stolen the lands of widows and orphans,
with having wasted the country and destroyed the
inhabitants, after cruelly harassing them. He ac-

TRIAL OF WARREN HASTINGS IN WESTMINSTER HALL

From rare mezzotint, engraved and published by R. Pollard, Jan. 18, 1789

cused him of never dining without creating a famine, of feeding on the indigent, the dying, and the dead. His cruelty, he said, was more revolting than his corruption ; and finally he ridiculed him as a swindler who had obtained honor under false pretenses. Low, mean, and contemptible as was his origin, bred in vulgar and ignoble habits, he became more proud than persons born to the imperial purple. Tyrant, thief, robber, cheat, swindler, sharper, a spider in Hell — all these he was, and more ; and finally the orator expressed his regret that the English language did not afford terms adequate to the enormity of his offenses.

The speech lasted four days, and affected different people in different ways. Those who were against Hastings thought it magnificent, said so, and hailed Burke as the modern Demosthenes. "Females" fainted at hearing of so hideous a monster, and had to be carried from the scene. Not all were of this opinion, however : honest Jim Burney, Fanny's brother, the sea-captain, protested that it was not eloquence at all, that it was mere rant, stuff, and nonsense, and that the whole thing was a comedy — nay, rather, a farce ; and Fanny, who agreed with him, told him to hush lest he should be overheard by Burke's son, who stood near them.

If the Lord Chancellor had called the formal charges "mere allegations," we can imagine with what scorn he listened to Burke's vituperations. It was at one of the sittings of this court, when Lord Thurlow was presiding, that Fox, struck by the solemnity of the Lord Chancellor's appearance, made his oft-quoted remark to a friend : "I wonder whether anyone ever was as wise as Thurlow looks ?"

If the law were, as it is sometimes said to be, that which is vehemently asserted and forcibly maintained, or if eloquence were evidence, the trial might well have been brought to an end then and there; but in point of fact the curtain had just been raised on a performance that was destined to continue for years, until the audience finally grew tired and went home, leaving the actors playing to empty benches.

But it must be confessed that there never had been a more brilliant first act, and never had play a greater cast. The next day, when Sheridan took the centre of the stage, it must have been quite obvious to him that, if he were to live up to his reputation as the greatest wit of the day, he would have to speak briefly and to the point. He did not dare attempt to outdo Burke in length, but he thought that perhaps he might be more forceful; he compressed, therefore, his speech into two days, and employed what was described at the time as something between poetry and prose and better than either. It was in this speech that Sheridan made his famous remark about the "luminous," which he subsequently corrected to "voluminous," page of Gibbon. And one may be quite sure that he, the great dramatist, the creator of the screen scene in the "School for Scandal," lost no opportunity for dramatic effect. In closing, he gathered himself up for a mighty effort, and pouring out his wrath and scorn on the "hideous and ignominious" figure before him, contrived to fall exhausted, almost fainting, into the outstretched arms of Burke. Altogether, it was magnificent team-work.

Fox, when his turn came, did not create, or, rather, maintain a good impression. He seemed at ease and in good humor for a moment, then fell into a passionate fit of vehemence, and as suddenly resumed his careless and disengaged air. On the whole, he was not convincing. Twenty years later one of this trio, Sheridan, tried to apologize to Hastings in an off-hand way, saying, "Of course you know we public speakers are expected to employ telling effects; it's our business." But Hastings would not admit the necessity, and ignored his outstretched hand. Of his feelings during all these torrents of oratory, he has left a record. "I was bewildered and for a time fascinated," he said, "by the immense vigor and energy with which I was attacked, and felt for half an hour the most culpable man on earth; but the feeling passed, and I knew in my heart that I was innocent of the infamous charges brought against me."

It could not be expected that society would forever give over all its customary amusements to attend a trial, however famous. For a time it was the talk of the town. But a theatrical tempest soon becomes wearisome; stage thunder and stage lightning seldom kill. Hastings had been admitted to bail, he moved about in society undisturbed, he bought the Daylesford estate, and took a town house in Park Lane. At intervals the trial went on; it was a long, tedious, and costly proceeding.

We know upon unimpeachable authority how observing a young woman was Fanny Burney, at that time second Keeper of the Robes to Queen Charlotte, with a residence at Windsor. At first Fanny was delighted at the privilege of attending the sittings at Westminster Hall, and she stored up in her mind all the interesting or amusing incidents, for recital when she got home; for the King, as he told her, preferred her narrative to any other; but gradually her interest, too, waned. The submission of long and complicated evidence is never an interesting proceeding for the on-looker, and week after week, and month after month, and year after year, it continued. She would have liked to be excused from further attendance, and suggested that the Hall was draughty and that she might catch cold; but the Queen told her to "wrap up well." It amused the King to listen to her account of the proceedings, and Majesty's wishes must be gratified.

What had at first been looked upon as the most important event of a reign full of interesting, dramatic, and scandalous incidents became at last an awful bore; and as it gave no promise of ever coming to an end, actors and audience alike became desperate. Hastings cried, "For God's sake end the matter one way or another; the expense is ruinous." "The Managers" had the public treasury behind them; but as Hastings was obliged to defray his expenses out of his own pocket, bankruptcy stared him in the face. Several years elapsed before his side had an opportunity to present its argument; and when finally Edward Law came to be heard, he gave by way of introduction the entire history of English affairs in India. It was probably the first and only clear and consecutive account of what the trial really was about. The "trash and rubbish," as Thurlow called the arguments presented by "the Managers," was designed to bewilder and befog rather than to enlighten the group of gouty old gentlemen assembled in all their magnificence to hear and sift the evidence presented to them.

Not being a Philadelphia lawyer, I have been unable to discover upon what theory the trial proceeded. Who were the judges? The peers of the realm, it would seem. Were they required to hear, or did they even pretend to hear, the evidence? Not after a little. Were they constant in their attendance? No. It so happened that, as the trial progressed, death took them, at first one by one, and then by little groups, and their places were taken by others; so that many who heard the defense of Hastings knew little and cared less about the attack that had been made upon him several years before. Indeed, it would appear that, although the legal machinery of the nation had been set in motion, it was not, in the usual sense, a trial at law at all.

The lawyers who entered into the proceeding did so because they saw an immense opportunity for fame and fortune. That was not a bad idea of Frederick, yclept the Great, that, if the lawyers about him could not settle a difficulty in court within a year from the time they began, then he would step in and settle it out of hand. Curiously, the rewards for non-success at the bar are frequently greater than those crowning successful effort. What other profession is so fortunate? A doctor makes a mistake and the patient dies — then and there is an end; but when the lawyer makes a mistake, he merely makes a motion for a new trial or takes the case to a higher court, and asks for a further retainer. I have a friend who takes a legal decision as reverently as Moses took the Ten Commandments on the top of Mount Ararat — if that was the name of the mountain from which "Thou shalt not" was sent reverberating through the ages. I once heard him say, "The joy of the law — " I would permit him to go no further. "The joy of the law," I interrupted, "is in writing briefly, 'To Services Rendered,' having in mind the sum your client is likely to have in bank, and doubling it." But this is a digression.

No student of eighteenth-century affairs will neglect the caricaturist; these men held up to nature a distorting glass, in which everything is out of focus, but which nevertheless emphasizes what is especially characteristic. During much of the time when Hastings was in the public eye, the public was too much interested in the notorious escapades of the Prince of Wales with the beautiful Mrs. Fitzherbert to care very much what became of the former Governor-General of India. Nevertheless, caricatures anent the trial were numerous, most of them being favorable to the prisoner. One, entitled the "Last Scene of the Managers' Farce," answers the very natural question, What has become of Philip Francis all this time? It represents Hastings rising in glory from the clouds of calumny, while Burke and Fox are in despair at the failure of their efforts; and behind is the crafty face of Francis, that malevolent *deus ex machina*, with the legend, "No character in the farce, but very useful behind the scenes."

LETTERS
FROM
SIMPKIN THE SECOND,
TO HIS
DEAR BROTHER IN WALES;
CONTAINING
AN HUMBLE DESCRIPTION OF THE TRIAL
OF
WARREN HASTINGS, Esq.
FROM THE COMMENCEMENT TO THE CLOSE OF THE
SESSIONS IN 1789.
WITH
NOTES AND ALTERATIONS BY THE AUTHOR.

To which are added,
SEVERAL LETTERS IN ANSWER, FROM
SIMON, AUNT BRIDGET, AND SHENKIN.
AND AN ORIGINAL POETICAL DEDICATION
TO THE RIGHT HON. EDMUND BURKE.
BY SIMPKIN.

THE SECOND EDITION.

LONDON:

PRINTED BY
JOHN BELL, British Library, STRAND,
Bookseller to His Royal Highness the Prince of Wales.
M DCC XCII.

What purported to be a series of "Letters from Simpkin the Second in London to his Dear Brother in Wales," an amusing skit written in doggerel, was much in vogue during the early years of the trial. Even Royalty enjoyed it. The salient features of the amusing spectacle were cleverly brought out, and it is clear that from the beginning Burke had the laboring oar. Difficulties as to the admissibility

of evidence consumed days, weeks at a time, as well
they might, when acts committed in India many years
before, and documents in outlandish tongues, were presented for the consideration of peers whose one idea
was to escape the rattle of words that pervaded Westminster Hall.   Burke

> affected to treat as a joke
> The doctrine of evidence written by Coke:
> And of all the absurdities he ever saw,
> The greatest absurdities were in the law.

His effort to create the belief that so high a tribunal
ought not to be bound by the forms and rules of evidence which obtain in ordinary trials gave some peer
an opportunity to make an obvious pun, that the
trial must be conducted according to "Law" — Law,
it may be remembered, being the name of Hastings's
chief counselor.

At length, the trial became, not only a bore, but a
scandal : somehow or other it had to be brought to an
end.   Other political issues had come to the fore, and
that which once seemed so important had entirely
lost its interest.   In France there was a revolution —
a King and Queen had been executed, and Burke's
intense passion for justice took another tangent.   At
home there had been too much of what we should
now call destructive criticism.   It was time to tighten
things up a bit; perhaps the shadow of the great Bon-
aparte was beginning to rest upon England.   *Be this
as it may*, it was time for the curtain to fall; the question was, who should ring it down?

It would seem that the peers finally came to the

rescue, not of Hastings, but of themselves. They at last began to take counsel together as to the mode of giving judgment. The trial, as Lord Thurlow, no longer Chancellor, said, had no parallel in history. It had extended over seven years and three months. Very little "evidence" had been presented. Hastings had been treated rather like a horse-thief than like one who had seen princes prostrate at his feet and nations obeying his commands. Reflections of this kind were inevitable, as it was seen that by no possibility could a verdict against him be secured.

No longer did Hastings appear a monster in human form; his hour of triumph was at hand. Once again he was formally called to the bar; he knelt down, and was bidden to rise and withdraw. The Lord Chancellor then put the question, "Is Warren Hastings, Esquire, guilty or not guilty?" The charges seem to have resolved themselves into fifteen; on two of them, bribery and corruption, he was unanimously acquitted. On the others, most of the lords, standing uncovered with their right hands upon their breasts, declared, "Not guilty upon my honor." There were some who voted guilty, but these adverse voters ranged only from two to five on various counts — very far from the majority required to convict. Lord Mansfield held him "not guilty" on all counts but one, and that concerned a question, not of justice but of the law, a seeming admission that justice and law are not synonymous. *La commedia è finita!*

It was for Hastings a complete vindication. The Managers had fallen out and were quarreling among themselves; the farce was over. It remained only to deliver the epilogue; it was brief and to the point, for the audience was impatient. "Warren Hastings, to the bar! You are acquitted of all things contained in the articles of impeachment. You are therefore discharged, *paying your own fees.*" Warren Hastings bowed and retired, an innocent man and a bankrupt. The great trial was at an end.

I sometimes think that the trial of Herr William Hohenzollern, had it taken place, would have been as great a farce. He has already been tried before the bar of public opinion of the world, and convicted. Why go through the motions of a trial? What punishment could be adequate to his crimes — other than to allow him, on some Devil's Island, to meditate upon them forever, if that were possible?

Since my interest in Warren Hastings has taken possession of me, much Hastings material has drifted from across the seas to a Daylesford the existence of which would have surprised and pleased the great man: portraits, documents, letters formal and letters friendly, cards of admission to the great spectacle; and some day, if I am patient, I may own that fine old mezzotint, "A view of the tryal of Warren Hastings, Esquire, before the Court of Peers in Westminster Hall."[1] Not a work of art perhaps, but what

---

[1] I wrote to Maggs Brothers, the great dealers in London, and asked if they had or could procure for me, a copy of this rare print. They replied that they had not one, but that if I only wished to examine it, they felt quite certain that the distinguished collector, Hampton L. Carson, Esq., of Philadelphia, would be glad to show me his; that Mr. Carson had "everything." I consulted Mr. Carson, found that

a human document! Marking curiously and quaintly an incident, on the whole creditable, in the life of
a great nation. For, absurd and grotesque as in
many respects the trial was, the ground for it was,
nevertheless, the maladministration of affairs in India, and it might properly be regarded as an attack
upon a corrupt and cruel system rather than upon an
individual. And good came of it. The proper government of dependencies was from that time assumed
as a national duty.

Before Hastings died, Parliament gave him in some
degree the honor that should long before have been
his. In 1813, his advice on Indian affairs was sought;
and upon his entrance the House of Commons rose
and uncovered — a most unusual proceeding. He
was listened to closely, and treated with great
respect. At the close of his examination the House
again rose and stood silent as he withdrew. Subsequently he was received and treated with the same
great courtesy by the Lords. He had become a great
historic figure.

he had indeed "everything," except the print I wanted. Again I
wrote to Maggs, leaving a standing order. Two years passed. I was
in London. One evening about tea-time, happening to be strolling
with my wife in the Charing Cross Road, we passed an old print
shop. "Why do you not inquire for your Hastings Trial?" said she.
We entered, and disturbing an old man at his tea, I put the question.
Wiping his mouth on his sleeve, he paused and then said, "I have
it, I'm trying to localize it. If you will stop in to-morrow morning,
I'll have it for you." "Are you certain?" I asked, quite willing to
spend the night there. "Quite." Needless to say, I was on hand
early next morning, and when, on being shown the print, a superb copy,
"proof before title," I asked the price, I was informed that he would
have to ask me £3 for it, at $3.50 to the pound! I was almost ashamed
to take it.

Throughout his long life Hastings carried himself with great dignity and reserve. The first shock of the impeachment proceedings over, he assumed the rôle of the philosopher, one which he was well fitted by nature to play. Immense power had been his; he had governed, and on the whole with justice and wisdom, an empire the extent and importance of which was at the time little understood. Expecting to be rewarded as others had been who had served their country faithfully, he was prosecuted like a criminal. He did not allow it greatly to disturb him, but went quietly about his affairs as if nothing was going to happen. He set about improving his Daylesford estate, at the same time residing during the season at his establishment in Park Lane, the leasehold of which he had secured in Mrs. Hastings's name. The house, then known as No. 1, was at the northern end of the street overlooking Hyde Park — a most desirable location. Subsequently, it became the town residence of Lord Rosebery, great-grandfather of the present Earl. In connection with the transfer of the property, there is some amusing correspondence. Lord Rosebery was not wealthy, but was in some way allowed to take possession of the house before he had signed an agreement or paid a deposit. Hastings, on hearing this, wrote to his banker: "Your letter has done what impeachment could not do — it has broken my rest. If his Lordship has possession, nothing but a law-suit in Chancery can force him to pay, should he go back on his bargain." Fortunately, all went well, and the house a hundred

years later passed by purchase into the hands of
George Murray Smith, of the firm of Smith, Elder &
Co., the publishers.

It was at Daylesford that Hastings spent the afternoon and evening of his long and eventful life. He
wrote poetry, and doubtless would have written, had
he, instead of Browning, thought of it,—

> Grow old along with me!
> The best is yet to be. The last
> Of life, for which the first was made.

Hastings said that the purchase of Daylesford en-
tailed a longer negotiation than would have served
for the acquisition of a province. It became a passion with him to build and plant, and Daylesford
House was erected in a park of some six hundred
acres. It was a large and comfortable mansion, fur-
nished with the gifts and acquisitions of a long and
distinguished life.

At the close of the trial Hastings, as has been said,
was, to all intents and purposes, a ruined man financially. The government did nothing for him, but
the East India Company, which he had served so
loyally, came to his aid, and advanced him large
sums, to be repaid at his convenience, without interest; and these debts were subsequently canceled.
He declined, with proper acknowledgments, the offer
of a pension of two thousand pounds per annum
from an Indian potentate; but he felt that he need
have no scruples in accepting from the Company
such sums as he required to enable him to live in

what seemed to him a fitting manner. In a communication to the Directors, he confessed that he had lived beyond his means, adding that strict "œconomy" could not be expected from one who had devoted his entire life to public affairs. It is indeed curious that, at a time when pensions were freely paid to the sisters and the cousins and the aunts of departed statesmen, as well as living politicians, nothing could be spared from the public or privy purse for such a man as Hastings. Whatever was needed, however, he had, and he continued to live, dispensing hospitality accompanied by sleep-inducing poetry, for many years — years that were probably the happiest of his life.

Every man is to a greater or less extent a dual personality. Hastings was a dreamer as well as a man of action. As a lad, to muse was, he says, his favorite recreation. "One summer's day, when I was scarcely seven years old, I well remember that I first formed the determination to buy back Daylesford. I was then literally dependent upon those whose condition scarcely raised them above the pressure of absolute want; yet somehow, as it did not appear unreasonable at the moment, so in after years it never faded away. God knows there were periods in my career when to accomplish that, or any other object of honorable ambition, seemed impossible, but I have lived to accomplish it. And though, perhaps, few public men have had more right than I to complain of the world's usage, I can never express sufficient gratitude to the kind Providence which

WARREN HASTINGS OF DAYLESFORD HOUSE, ESQUIRE

permits me to pass the evening of a long, and I trust not a useless life, amid scenes that are endeared to me by so many personal as well as traditional associations."

At what time he dreamed of England's greatness in India, he does not tell us; but he lived to see that dream, too, come true; and forceful, nay, brutal, as he undoubtedly was in India, so kindly and gentle was he to his wife, by whom he was survived for twenty years — years devoted to his memory.

With Daylesford in Pennsylvania, I am much at home. Life in our little hamlet is not unduly stimulating. Such local happenings as occasionally find their way into the newspapers are generally occasioned by a sharp and dangerous turn in the much-traveled Lancaster Pike, an old post-road, now taking the grander name of the Lincoln Highway. This road, plunging under the railway bridge just at the station, appears to be going in one direction, whereas it is actually going in another. Not all automobilists know this, and two or more of them trying to occupy the same space at the same time afford all the excitement we seem to require. Twenty-five years' residence has made few changes other than that, speaking to our trees and to our children, we can truthfully say, "How you have grown!"

Daylesford in Worcestershire I visited when I was last in England, and I had the pleasure of being shown over the entire estate by its present owner, Squire Young, a kindly gentleman much resembling

Cardinal Newman in appearance. But the interest at Daylesford is the church rather than the house. I was traveling with that exquisite book of Le Gallienne's, "Travels in England," by way of a guide; opening it I read: "Almost as soon as you catch sight of it [the church] from the road, you see, too, a great urn standing over a tomb beneath the east window. Something tells you that that is the tomb you seek, and, when you reach it, you find engraven upon it the words 'Warren Hastings,' simply as they are engraved across the Indian Empire, though perhaps hardly so everlastingly. As one turned and looked round at the peaceful green hills on every side, it seemed strange to think what thundering avenues of fame converged at this point of quiet grass."

The original church dated back a thousand years or so — one "fabrick" giving away to another; the one now standing was built at a time when English architecture — and our own — was at its very worst: 1860. It supersedes a small and simple structure erected by the great old man in an effort, it may be, to make his peace with Heaven. A tablet erected in the former church, now removed into the present structure, testifies in a long inscription, "To the eminently virtuous and lengthened life of Warren Hastings, Esquire, of Daylesford House in this Parish, first Governor General of the British territories in India," etc., ending with the pious hope, in which we join, that the soul of the Lord's departed servant may be at peace.

II

My life has always been a singularly duplex affair: one half of it — no, much more, nine tenths of it — has been hard work, the rest of it has been spent in my library; even when I was a boy and had only a shelf or two of books, I always called it my library.

As a result of much reading,— and very little thinking; for like Charles Lamb, books do my thinking for me,— I became moved to write a paper on the pleasure of buying and owning books; and, much to my delight, not only was it accepted by a well-known editor, paid for, and published, but people read it and asked for more. It is the first step *qui coûte*, as the French so eloquently say. After the acceptance of my first article my ascent was easy.

I have said that I have always been misunderstood. For example: I never had any education, whereas it is commonly supposed that I have sat, or at least stood, at the knee of some great scholar like Kittredge. The fact is that kindly disposed relatives took me in hand at an early age and sent me from one dame — I had almost said damn — school to another, according to the views of the one who had me in charge for the time being. This is a bad plan.

In like manner, when I grew up I got a job in a bookstore, Porter & Coates's, and a fine bookstore it was; but I never sold any books.   I suppose it was early discovered that, though I might take a customer's money, I would never part with the books, never deliver the goods, as it were, and for that reason I was put in the stationery department.   I made my first acquaintance with pens, ink, and paper by selling them, and in those days I had no idea what delightful playthings they make.   Because I spent a few years at Porter & Coates's, I am supposed to have gained there the knowledge of books that I am credited with.

And later on I was for a time in a banking-house, and a most respectable banking house it was, too: Brown Brothers & Co. — a sort of younger son of Brown, Shipley & Co. of London.   There I drew bills of exchange in sets of three: first, second, and third of exchange, I remember they were called.   I never became much of a draftsman, but I soon became expert enough to make three separate blunders in a single bill.   It took time for these blunders to come to the surface.   I made a mistake in June in Philadelphia, and it came to light in Shanghai in December.   I used to dread the arrival of a steamer. I did not mind "steamer day"—that meant outgoing mail; what I hated was an incoming post.   I can see now the brief notes written in clerkly longhand,— it was before the introduction of typewriters in respectable houses,— "calling attention for the sake of regularity to the error in draft" — number, name, and amount given.   I came to know just how long after the arrival of the mail it would be before someone would tell me that Mr. Delano wanted to see me in the back office.

This was the unhappiest time of my life. I can imagine nothing more miserable than to spend the best part of one's life in counting money, especially some other fellow's money. Dr. Johnson, once reproached for his clumsiness in counting money, remarked, "But, Sir, consider how little experience I have had." I had had as little. Then, to make the game more difficult and to add to my misery, I was expected to count it, not only in dollars and cents, but in pounds, shillings, pence, francs, marks, and anything else that the devilish ingenuity of man could contrive. Reflection told me that I not only was in the wrong pew, but in the wrong church as well; I determined to throw up my job and go into business for myself: to do in a wholesale way what I had done at retail. After some years, when I had accumulated a little money, a man, thinking I had much, called on me with a view to selling me an interest in an electrical business. I was told that what was needed was a financial manager; and when upon investigation I discovered that the business was in the hands of the sheriff, I knew that I had not been deceived.

A story of suffering and disaster is usually more interesting than a story of commonplace success. How in time I became the president of an electrical manufacturing company, without knowing a volt from an ampere, or a kilowatt from either, might be interesting to my family, had they not heard it before, but to no one else. It is enough for me to say that by the happiest kind of a fluke I came to have a name not quite unknown in electrical and financial circles, although nothing of an electrical engineer and very little of a financier.

And now in my old age,— for if an electrical business will not prematurely age a man, nothing will,— when I sometimes so far forget myself as to talk of eddy currents and hysteresis, I see that I deceive no one; that I am listened to as an old man is, when for the hundredth time he starts to tell what he thinks is a funny story; for I am known to hate every living mechanical thing with a royal hatred — automobiles especially, with their thousand parts, each capable of being misunderstood. Even a screw-driver fills me with suspicion, and a monkey-wrench with horror.

And I am not altogether alone in this : others so situated share my weakness. I was dining once in London, quite informally, with a great electrical engineer, a very trig maid in attendance. On the table near my host's right hand was a small block of white marble and a tiny silver mallet. When he wanted the maid, he struck the marble a resounding blow.

I was somewhat amused, and asked him if he had ever heard of a push-button for the same purpose.

"My boy, I have," was his reply, "but I get enough of electrical devices in the city; I don't want a single one of them in my own home. I've not come yet to using gas; I prefer candles; they are not so likely to get out of order. I hate this pushing a dimple and waiting for something to happen. When I make a noise myself I begin to feel a sense of progress; that's what we stand for in this country," — with a knowing wink,— "progress."

I have frequently been asked how I came to write a book. It is one of the few questions that have been asked that I can answer. Away back in 1907 we had a panic; we have been in such a turmoil, financial and other, since, that some of us have forgotten the very respectable dimensions of the money panic of the autumn of 1907. Not so the writer. I had gone to Europe, in no way pleased with the financial outlook, and to some extent prepared for a breeze, but not for a typhoon. Enough: Christmas came as Christmas will, and when it came time to say a word of greeting, it seemed absurd to send a man (or a woman, for women sometimes suffer in panics just as much as men do) a dainty little card with a picture of a bunch of mistletoe or a reindeer pulling a sleigh, and wishing him or her a "Merry Christmas." Admitting that "merriment" is a conventional wish anyway, I could not bring myself to do it.

While I was turning over in my mind whether it would not be possible for me to hit upon some thought which might raise a smile amid the general gloom, and for a moment escape the waste-paper basket, I chanced to drop in on Horace Traubel, who, having little to lose, was as happy as ever; and in looking over his Whitman manuscripts I came across a scrap of paper on which was written a sentiment that seemed particularly appropriate to the moment. So I had a facsimile of it made and printed on one side

of a card, with my own comment on the other. This
provided me with a "greeting" that caught the fancy
of some of my friends. Several "Captains" of politics,
industry, and finance, to whom it was shown, wrote
me and asked if I could "spare a copy"; and almost
immediately my supply was exhausted and the matter passed out of my mind until the next year, when
I again indulged myself in a greeting a little more
personal than could be bought in a shop. I have continued this practice since : thus my descent into literature was gradual and easy.

Quite recently, in the drawer of an unused desk, I
found a sole remaining copy of my Christmas card
of 1907, which I now reproduce.

To the courtesy of Mr. Horace Traubel I am indebted
for the opportunity of reproducing an interesting scrap of
Whitman's handwriting. In Traubel's recently published
book, "With Walt Whitman in Camden,"— one of the
most remarkable biographical works since Boswell's
"Johnson,"— we read that he (Traubel) one day picked
up from the floor of Whitman's little study a stained piece
of paper and, reading it, looked at Whitman rather quiz-
zically. "What is it?" he asked. I handed it to him.
He pushed his glasses down over his eyes and read it.
"That's old and kind o' violent — don't you think — for
me? Yet I don't know but it still holds good."

If this was true twenty years ago, how much truer is it
to-day? And if it be said that Whitman was extreme in
his views and unguarded in his writings, what may be said
of the following absurdity redeemed by wit : —

"He touched the dead corpse of public credit," said
Daniel Webster of Alexander Hamilton, "and it sprung
upon its feet."

Go on, my dear Americans,
whip your horses to the utmost—
excitement! money! politics!—open
all your valves and let her go—swing,
whirl with the rest—you will soon
get under such momentum you can't
stop if you would). Only make pro-
vision (return, old States) and new
States, for several thousand insane
asylums. You are in a fair way
to create a whole nation of lunatics.

Walt Whitman

REPRODUCTION FROM A WHITMAN MANUSCRIPT, USED BY A. E. N. AS A
CHRISTMAS CARD, 1907

Is it to be said of another New York Federalist, infinitely more popular and far more of a Federalist than Hamilton, that he touched the healthy body of private credit and it became a corpse? Shall it be added that an adoring nation cheered the miracle and murmured with reverent lips: "Hail, Cæsar! We who are about to bust salute you"?

Or of the following absurdity unredeemed:—

"All that our people have to do now is to go ahead with their normal business in a normal fashion and the whole difficulty disappears; and this end will be achieved at once if each man will act as he normally does act. . . .

"The Government will see that the people do not suffer if only the people themselves will act in a normal way."

No mollycoddle's work is this; this broad guaranty drips clumsily from the pen of a strenuous man in a panic at the panic he has made.

Under "normal" conditions it would now be in order to shout Merry Christmas and A Happy New Year; but to shout anything at the moment might be out of place — thanks to our so-called "Captains" of Politics, Industry, and Finance, a Merry Christmas is out of the question, and a Happy New Year unlikely.

Cheer up. Let's have a drink: "Here's to a full baby-carriage and an empty dinner-pail!"

A. E. N.

Times change quickly, and once again we face an era of the empty dinner-pail. Whose fault is it? How shall it be remedied? These are not questions for the mere book-collector, for the nonce (how long is a nonce?) wielding a pen.

Do not be alarmed, gentle reader; this introduction is almost over. It is like a door stuck tight which, when, by a great effort, you have forced it open, you find leads nowhere.

I set out some time ago to tell how I came to be an author, and then I lost my place; better authors than I ever hope to be have done the same.

I shall start over again. There is a rhyme to this effect: —

> A little home well filled,
> A little wife well willed,
> Are great riches.

Having these, I wanted one thing more. I wanted to add a leaf — I did not ask to add a tree, not even a sapling, only a single leaf — to that forest which we call English literature, that stately forest in which for many years I have delighted to lose myself. It is an honorable ambition and I gave it full play; and I was as pleased as Punch when, after a time, it was suggested that if, in addition to a number of essays that had already appeared in the "Atlantic," I had some other literary material, as it is called, it would be read with the idea of publication in book form.

In due time a book appeared — a book, mind you. Boswell, in conversation one day with Johnson, remarked that he had read a certain statement. "Why, Sir, no doubt," replied the sage, "but not in a bound book." There is a great difference between an essay in a magazine and the same essay in a bound book. My book was bound. As one of my critics very kindly said of the publication, it might not be worthy of the immortality of morocco, but it certainly was a very pretty success "in boards."

But, after all, reading is the test. Anyone can write and print and bind a certain number of pages;

the thing is to get people to read them. A great man
can wait for posterity, but for a little man it is now
or never. A book's life is almost as brief as a butter-
fly's. There is something pathetic about the brevity
of the life of a book. A man works over it, thinks
about it, talks about it, if he can get anyone to listen
to him; at last he finds a publisher, and the book appears. For a few days, perhaps, it may be seen in the
bookshops, and then, like the snowflake in the river,
it disappears, and forever. Speaking by and large,
the greatest successes escape this fate only for a moment. There are so many books! Go into any public
library and ask what proportion of the books on the
shelves are called for, say, once in ten years. The
answer should make for modesty in authors. That it
does not do so proves only with what eagerness we
pursue the phantoms of hope.

But I must avoid a minor note in my carol. D'Is-
raeli has written of the Calamities and Quarrels of
authors — I write only of the amenities of authorship. When writing ceases to be a delight, I will give
it over. Meanwhile, the trifling honor that has come
to me is very gratifying. My book was published in
November, 1918. Within a short time commenda-
tory letters began to arrive. They came from every
part of the country, at first single spies, and then bat-
talions. Almost all of them from entire strangers.
Not many of my friends wrote me. When a man is
publishing his first book, his friends, feeling that a
great joke is being perpetrated, want to have a hand
in it and do not hesitate to remind him that they are

looking forward to receiving a presentation volume, the inference being that they, at least, may be depended upon to read it. But I remembered Dr. Johnson's remark: "Sir, if you want people to read your book, do not give it to them. People value a book most when they buy it."

When the book finally appeared, and people began to read and talk of it, many things, grave as well as gay, resulted, the gayest being a dinner given to me at one of the clubs, at which I was presented with a copy of my own book superbly bound by Zucker in full crushed levant morocco. A special page was inserted in it, whereon was printed, among other gibes and floutings, a paragraph from the book itself: "I trust my friends will not think me churlish when I say that it is not my intention to turn a single copy of this, my book, into a presentation volume." This was followed by a "*stinging rebuke* from the uncommercial committee which is paying for the dinner and which regards presentation copies as the cardinal virtue of good book-collecting."

It was a merry dinner, and well on toward morning, after the wine had been flowing freely for several hours, my friend Kit Morley wrote on the back of a menu card the following parody of Leigh Hunt's well-known poem, "Abou Ben Adhem": —

ABOU A. EDWARD

A. Edward Newton — may his tribe e'er wax —
Awoke one night from dreaming of Rosenbach's,
And saw among the bookshelves in his room,
Making it like a "Shelley first" in bloom,

Abou A. Edward

A. Edward Newton — may his tribe e'er wax.
Awoke one night from dreaming of Rosenbach's
And saw among the bookshelves in his room,
Making it like a 'Shelley first' in bloom
A boswell writing in a book of gold.
Amenities had made Ben Edward bold
And to the vision in the room, he said
"What writest thou?" the boswell raised its head
And with a voice almost as stern as Hector's,
Replied. "An index of the great collectors."
"Sir,
am I one?" quoth Edward. "Nay, not so,"
Replied the Boswell. Edward spake more low
But cheerly still "Sir, let us have no nonsense!
Write me at least as a lover of Dr. Johnson's."
The Boswell wrote and vanished. The next night
He came again with an increase of light
And shewed the names whom love of books had blessed —
And lo, A. Edward's name led all the rest!

                              Leigh Hunt
                                 per CM

PARODY OF A FAMOUS POEM, BY CHRISTOPHER MORLEY

A Boswell writing in a book of gold.
Amenities had made Ben Edward bold,
And to the vision in the room he said,
"What writest thou?" The Boswell raised its head,
And with a voice almost as stern as Hector's,
Replied, "An index of the great collectors."
"Sir, am I one?" quoth Edward. "Nay, not so,"
Replied the Boswell. Edward spake more low,
But cheerly still: "Sir, let us have no nonsense!
Write me at least as a lover of Dr. Johnson's."
The Boswell wrote and vanished. The next night
He came again with an increase of light,
And showed the names whom love of books had blessed —
And lo, A. Edward's name led all the rest!

In the cold gray light of the morning after, it was
seen that this poem lacks some of those transcendent
qualities which have given Shelley's "Cloud" and
Keats's "On First Looking into Chapman's Homer"
such enduring fame; but at the time it was composed
and read, it produced a prodigious effect upon the
company, and some day my heirs, executors, admin-
istrators, and assigns may sell the manuscript at auction for a price which will amaze them. — But this
verges upon prophecy.

I had another pleasant experience not long after
the publication of the "Amenities," to which I refer
chiefly that I may link my name, if only for a moment, with that of a dear friend and fine scholar, now
dead, Francis B. Gummere.

I was in Boston, and had been invited to a meal,
too elaborate to be called a luncheon and hardly formal enough for a dinner, at the Club of Odd Volumes,
as the guest of George Parker Winship, the librarian

of the Widener Memorial Library. It was a delightful affair, and I was seated next to a good Johnsonian, Mr. Harold Murdock, who was good-naturedly chaffing me over some item which I had wanted and he had acquired at a recent sale, when a distinguished-looking man entered the room and took his place at the other end of the table. Hearing that there was merriment at our end, he joined in the good-natured raillery, and I, having no idea who he was, seized upon what appeared to be a good opening to say: "You're having a good deal of fun at my expense; you have the advantage of me — you know who I am: I am a distinguished guest; whereas I do not know you at all; you may be a man of no import—"

The rest of my sentence was lost in a burst of laughter, at the end of which he told me he was George L. Kittredge, and I discovered that I was bandying words with a landmark of learning at Harvard, and by common consent the most distinguished professor of English in the country. I had to carry matters with a high hand, or I should have been done for. So I told him not to apologize and that I seemed to remember having heard my friend Gummere speak highly of him. "Ah," replied Kittredge, "do you know Gummere?" And when I told him that I did, he, like the polished gentleman that he is, rose and, filling his wine-glass, bowed and said, "Sir, I am drinking wine *with you and to him.*"

Well, we spent a delightful afternoon together,— at least it was delightful to me,— in the course of which Kittredge said: "Did you ever meet a man

THE LATE FRANCIS B. GUMMERE,
PROFESSOR OF ENGLISH AT HAVERFORD COLLEGE

more universal in his knowledge than Frank? What
a delightful companion he is! Have you ever heard
of a book that he has not read?"

And then I told him of a little club of which I had
been a member for thirty years or more, a club without a name or rules or anything, which it was difficult to get into, and once in, impossible to get out of,
of which my friends Henry Hanby Hay[1] and H. H.
Bonnell and Felix Schelling were the founders, and
which Gummere finally joined as our baby member.
It's a thing of the past now, our club; but what a
club it was! We devoted ourselves to the study of
the more obscure English authors. There was plenty
of give and take at our meetings, and it was an established custom among us, when we saw a head, to hit
it. At our meetings how Gummere shone! And when
he forgot himself, as he occasionally did, and overwhelmed us with his learning, it was our habit to
bring him down to earth by saying, "Steady there,
Gummere, remember you are not Kittredge!"

When our sitting broke up, as sittings must, at
parting Kittredge said to me, "When you see Frank,
give him my love. He's one of my oldest and warm-
est friends."

On my way home a day or two later, I chanced to
pick up a paper and read that Gummere, the cultured,
amiable scholar, had suddenly passed away. I never
had an opportunity of delivering Kittredge's mes-

---

[1] I wish here and now formally to acknowledge the debt I owe to the
Club (especially to dear old Hay); and, paraphrasing Dick Steele, I
might say that to have been a member of it for thirty years is a liberal
education.

sage, and our little club has never had a meeting
since his death. I fancy it had outlived its usefulness;
most of us joined it when we were in our early twen-
ties, and we had, to quote Goldsmith's remark, which
so aroused Dr. Johnson's ire, "travelled pretty well
over one another's minds." Some of us were getting
too old to be regular in our attendance, and old Father
Time, too, had been busy with his scythe, and there
was a feeling that the places of those who had gone
could never be filled.

Written, as my book professedly was, for the tired
business man, it had an equal success with the sex
which we have been taught to think of as fair. I came
to have in some small measure the astonished feeling
that Byron had, when he awoke and found himself
famous, except that I feared to wake and discover
that my success was a dream. I dreaded the arrival
of the time when flattering letters would be a thing of
the past, and when friends would no longer stop me
in the street to tell me that they never would have
supposed that I could write a book.

My reputation as a Johnsonian grew out of all
proportion to my knowledge; and if I recast a bit of
dialogue with a casual acquaintance on a street corner it must stand, not for the single encounter, but
for a hundred.

FRIEND. — I never hear Dr. Johnson's name mentioned without thinking of you.

N. — That's very good of you (*with a leer*).

FRIEND.— There were two Johnsons were n't there?
Did n't one write plays?

N. — Yes, but they spelled their names differently, and Ben Jonson died —

FRIEND. — I remember I sat in his seat in a tavern the last time I was in London in 1907,— no, 1909, I can't remember now whether it was 1907 or 1909,— but I sat in Dr. Johnson's seat in a tavern; let me see, I have forgotten the name, but it was in the Strand.

N. (*wearily*). — No, it was not in the Strand, it was in Fleet Street, and the name of the tavern was the Cheshire Cheese —

FRIEND (*exultingly, as one who has found great treasure*). — That's it — the Cheshire Cheese! I had lunch there and I sat in Dr. Johnson's seat. Have you ever been there.

N. — Yes, and it may surprise you to know that there is not one single contemporary reference to Johnson's ever having visited the Cheshire Cheese.

FRIEND. — Why, that's queer. I was told —

N. (*firmly*). — Yes, I know very well what you were told, but it's all fiction. The legend that he frequently visited the Cheshire Cheese has grown up in the last century, and is founded on nothing more than possibility, or, at most, probability.

FRIEND. — You surprise me. Well, it's a dirty old place, anyhow. I always preferred going to Simpson's.

N. — Now you're talking! Don't you wish you were there now? Well, I must be on my way.

For the reason, I suppose, that it was soon recognized that my book was written in the leisure hours of a busy man, it escaped severe treatment at the hands of the critics. Allowances were made. Dr. Johnson suggests that a woman's preaching should not be criticized; rather, one should be surprised that she does it at all. Thus amiably was my writing considered. It was, however, rather disconcerting to discover that in no single instance, I believe, was I asked a question that I was able to answer. This leads me to reach the profound conclusion that there are many more questions than answers in this world.

One thing greatly surprised me: it seems that my book had created the very erroneous idea that all old books are valuable, especially those in which ∫'s take the place of s's. This form — which began almost with the art of printing, continued throughout the eighteenth century, and signifies exactly nothing at all — was supposed to be a mark of special significance; and it took all the tact I was master of to break the news of its lack of significance gently to those who were thinking of selling a few volumes which had long been regarded as invaluable family treasures.

When the famous Gutenberg Bible was bought by Mr. Huntington at the Hoe sale in New York, in 1911, people generally — especially in the remote country — formed the idea that, Mr. Gutenberg having recently died, his widow had disposed of the family Bible for the sum of fifty thousand dollars, and, it was thought, would be willing to pay a substantial fraction of this sum for any other old Bible that might be offered. Consequently, "Mrs. Gutenberg" was overwhelmed with offerings of Bibles, most of which would have been dear at one dollar.

In like manner, I was overwhelmed with offerings of Burns. I had casually mentioned, in speaking of a Kilmarnock Burns in boards uncut, that the price might be about five thousand dollars. The book was published in 1786, and the reasoning which went on in the minds of those who addressed me on the subject seems to have been: if a copy of Burns printed one hundred and twenty-five years ago is worth five thousand dollars, a copy half as old would be worth half as much; certainly a copy of Burns printed in 1825 must be worth, say, a thousand dollars.

One old lady, suffering from sciatica and desirous of spending some months at Mount Clemens, decided to part with her copy for this amount. She wrote me as follows: "My copy of Burns belonged to my grandfather. It is of 1825 edition, bound with gilt edges, and is in fair condition for so old a book (almost a hundred years). It is of course very yellow and some pages are much worn; *however, it is all there.*"

Another lady wrote: "Understanding you are desirous of buying old books, I write to say that I know of families having same in their possession. Before I make inquiry I want to get all the information possible. I am anxious to make money in a pleasing way, and this seems along the lines of my taste and inclinations. Please let me know what you want to buy, by return mail." Not getting a reply by return mail, she wrote another letter, this time sending a stamped envelope: "I wrote you recently about old books. I am anxious to begin. Please write at once, sending me a list of books that are valuable."

From a man in Texas came this gem, on a letter-head of William Crawford, who called himself an Electrician, Plumber, and Steamfitter: "Dear Sir: I understand you have gotten out a book giving a list of old books that are valuable. Does it come free of charge? If so, send it right along, as I know where some books are that I would like to know the value of."

Many of these tributes to my genius I owe to the editor of that enterprising journal, the Kansas City "Star," for an excellent review which appeared in that paper,— I call it excellent because it was so flattering,— and which was copied far and wide, even in the metropolitan press. It created the idea that I knew all that was to be known about the entrancing subject of book-collecting. "Get hold of a book entitled 'The Amenities of Book-Collecting,' by A. Edward Newton, and you will find therein the golden key that will open up for you whatever there is of mystery about the game," the review said.

This "golden-key" business bedeviled me for a time. I was asked to send forward promptly the "golden key," and at the time, not having seen the article, I was quite in the dark to know what was meant. It seemed as if, the moment this phrase met the eye of the reader, he or she followed the instructions *au pied de la lettre*. One man, evidently a business man in Minnesota with no time for the "Amenities," wrote me briefly and to the point: "Give me all particulars about old rare books. Send me the 'golden key' at once. I have some."

My prize letter, however, reached me in England. It is a pretty generally accepted opinion over there that every American is a millionaire, and when the English think of us, it is usually to call to mind the old adage about a fool and his money. My correspondent certainly did when he penned this gem: —

11 CLOVELLY ROAD, HORNSEY, LONDON,
October 30, 1920.

DEAR SIR: —

I have in my possession a book called "Catulli Tibulli et Propertii Opera," the works of Catullus, Tibullus, & Propertius, Latin poets, in Latin, published at London 1715 by Tonson & Watts. It has the following important inscription: "James Boswell Cambridge 1760. A Present from my friend Temple." You can have this extremely interesting memento of the famous friendship between Boswell and Temple for *one thousand pounds*.

As I understand from the "Bookman's Journal" that you are at present in London, I shall be pleased to wait upon you, if you so desire it, to show you the book. I have addressed this letter c/o your publisher, Mr. Lane.

Hoping to hear from you at your convenience, I am,

Yours v. truly,
PETER STRUTHERS.

Now think of it! But for the kindness of my correspondent, I might never have suspected that Catullus, Tibullus, and Propertius were Latin poets; and no doubt Mr. Struthers's mind was working normally when he assumed that an American would be willing to acquire the volume for a sum almost equal, at the normal rate of exchange, to five thousand dollars! Disappointed, he may by this time have sold his "interesting memento" to some dealer in the Charing Cross Road for a few shillings, and I may yet become the owner of it for a guinea, at which figure it would be by no means a bargain.

From the days of the Phœnicians the English have been fixing both the buying and the selling price. It is no accident, but industry directed by intelligence, that has made them the greatest traders in the world. If you doubt this statement, read "England's Treasure by Forraign Trade," by Thomas Mun; it was written almost three hundred years ago, but a modern reprint is readily obtainable. At the moment, they are in debt to us, and the idea is very distasteful to them; so distasteful that they propose that we should cancel our loans to them, in exchange for which courtesy they propose to cancel loans to their *insolvent* debtors to an equal amount. It sounds preposterous, but is it?

Europe, they say, cannot possibly pay its debts. I doubt if it can. The debt of the Allied nations to us is, roughly, ten billion dollars; the interest charge alone will soon amount to two million dollars a day! Think of it! Theoretically, the debt, both principal and interest, is payable in gold; actually, it must be paid in merchandise, for there is not enough gold to go round. Do we Americans want ten billion dollars' worth of manufactured goods or staples seeping into this country? Would not farmer and manufacturer

alike build a tariff wall to prevent it? And if we could
collect the money over a long term of years, should
we be wise to do so, thereby bankrupting our best
customer? Would it not be better to get down to
brass tacks, fund the debt, spread it over a term of
years, and pay it ourselves? We now know what it
costs to elect a president on the issue "He kep' us
out of war," when we should have been in it, and
the price of "Making the world safe for Democracy";
I, for one, maintain that it is not worth it.

There is only one mistake we have not yet made,
and that is, having finally become convinced that it
would be unwise or impossible to collect the debt, to
continue to hold it over our late allies and talk about
our generosity in not pushing our claim.

But to return to my correspondence, after this
brief foray into the dismal science.

I received some letters which would give delight
even to so hardened an author as H. G. Wells. Captains of Industry, whose names are household words
in Wall Street, seem to have found relief from the
cares of the hour in my pages; and officers just returned from duty in France, anxious to forget the
horrors of the Argonne, dipped into me as if I were a
bath of oblivion. Finally, I was asked to name my
price for lectures. Of the many unexpected results of
my little success, this was the most amusing. I invariably replied to requests for "terms" by a story
told me by Sir Walter Raleigh, the great Oxford
scholar. A friend, being asked to name his fee for a

lecture, replied, "I have a three-guinea lecture and a five-guinea lecture and a ten-guinea lecture, but I can't honestly recommend the three-guinea lecture." I said that I had only three-guinea lectures in stock and that I could n't recommend them, especially as I should have to charge a hundred guineas for them. No doubt my correspondents thought me mad.

It was Sir Walter Raleigh who suggested that I write a paper on Mrs. Thrale, although my title for it, "A Light-Blue Stocking," is my own. And speaking of Sir Walter, let me tell a story of him, which I have never seen in print, but which deserves to be immortal.

He was to deliver a series of ten-guinea lectures at Princeton University, and was expecting to be met by President Hibben at the railway station. Just at the hour of his arrival, Dr. Hibben discovered that he had a very important meeting of the trustees, or something, which he could not very well miss. There was nothing to be done but call upon one of the younger professors to go to the station, meet the distinguished man, and escort him to "Prospect," Dr. Hibben's residence.

The professor thus called upon was glad to be of service, but remarked, "I have never met Sir Walter. How shall I know him?"

"Oh, very easily," replied Dr. Hibben; "Sir Walter is a very large, distinguished-looking man. You can't miss him; you will probably know almost every man getting off the train from New York; the man you don't know will be the man you are looking for."

With these instructions Dr. Hibben's representative proceeded to the station, met the incoming train, and seeing a large, distinguished-looking man wearing a silk hat, approached him, remarking, "I presume I am addressing Sir Walter Raleigh."

The gentleman thus accosted was much astonished, but, pulling himself together, quickly replied, "No! I'm Christopher Columbus. You will find Sir Walter Raleigh in the smoking-car playing poker with Queen Elizabeth."

The man, as it turned out, was a New York banker; he had heard much of the impudence of the Princeton undergraduate and decided to nip it in the bud. No one enjoyed the story more than Sir Walter himself when it was told him.

In the words of "Koheleth," — as my friend Dr. Jastrow prefers to call the author of "Ecclesiastes," in his delightful book, "The Gentle Cynic," — "Hear the conclusion of the whole matter: 'Much study is weariness to the flesh.'" — "Much" study, observe. I have given my subject only such study as has produced, not weariness, but pleasure. Books are for me a solace and a joy. We are told that of the making of them there is no end. Be it so. Let us rejoice that, whatever comes, books will continue to be, books that suit our every mood and fancy. If all is vanity, as "The Preacher" says, how can we better employ our time than by reading books and writing about them?

III

LUCK

I AM a strong believer in luck. I know that Emerson says that luck is the refuge of the shallow, but I don't care much what one philospher says; I will find you another philosopher of equal standing who will flatly disagree. Gibbon, in his fascinating "Autobiography," speaks of his life as being the lucky chance of one unit against millions; and in proportion to my deserts I have been far luckier than he; but we can have too much of a good thing. I once heard a story of a man who, walking along a country road, noticed a horse-shoe lying at his feet, and, picking it up, remarked to himself, "I'm in luck." A few yards farther on he picked up another, saying as he did so, "This is certainly my lucky day." A little farther on he came across another, and then another, and he kept on picking them up until he was loaded down with them. Finally he saw, some distance ahead of him, a large wagon full of old, rusty horse-shoes, on its way to the junk-heap, which led him to make the wise observation that too much luck is junk.

In trudging along the dusty road of life, I have picked up symbols of luck just often enough to make me feel sure that they were not falling from an overloaded wagon. I was lucky when my wife picked me

out for her husband and so delicately ensnared me
that I thought I was doing the courting. My children have not been a bitter disappointment, and I
have been singularly blessed in the matter of a business partner. And finally, I wrote a book, the success of which I feel sure made even my friends admit
that I was right, at least once, when I said that my
achievements were largely — luck. How my book
came to be published was told in the introduction,
and need not be told over again. Nor am I now concerned with the impression it made on others; its
readers could work their way through its pages and
forget it, but its publication had a profound effect
upon its writer. It gave him a reputation as a collector so far above that which he merited that, in an
effort to live up to it, he has well-nigh ruined himself. We are so constituted that we never care to hear
much of the successes of our friends ; but their difficulties are very comforting to us, and, properly set
down, make very pretty reading; so I continue.

The foolish and ignorant frequently say to me:
"However do you find such lovely and wonderful
things?" "Lovely" and "wonderful" are the words
they use ; and when, in reply, I tell them that the difficulty is not in the finding but in the paying for such
treasures as I seem to require for my reputation's
sake, they think that I am spoofing them, to use a
word we have borrowed from our English cousins.

There is, of course, a certain class of literary property to which I have no right — items so far above
my means that they make no appeal whatever. I

remember once hearing an old gentleman of considerable means say, in reply to my question why he did not buy such and such things that I knew he would enjoy : "I would like to have them, of course ; but if I should buy them, what would the Vanderbilts buy ?" In like manner, assuming that the possession of a pocketful of Shakespeare quartos meant more to me than the possession of wife and children with a tight roof over our heads, and that I should yield to temptation, what would the real collectors do ?

But there are countless items in what may be called the second class, which formerly used to come my way and tempt me occasionally, but which now come in close formation. Such defense as I am able to make seems to have no effect whatever. If life is, as life is said to be, just one damn thing after another, what shall be said of my existence, temperamentally fitted to withstand everything except temptation ? And the arguments of my friends, the booksellers, are so skillfully brought to bear ; they scratch where it itches, and I am so grateful — until the first of the month, when the bills come in.

I had supposed that I could resist flattery. I have been selling something or other all my life. I know something of the wiles of the class to which I belong ; but since I first tried my prentice-hand at making a living by selling things, a class has grown up so skillful that I am — how does the old phrase go ? — but wax in their hands. Be this as it may, my ruin is impending — I know it is ; and when the sheriff gets me, as he surely will, and to satisfy my creditors my

books have to be sold, I have decided just what title
my friend Mitchell Kennerley, that genial soul who
presides over the fortunes of the Anderson Auction
Company in New York, will put upon my sales
catalogue : —

WHO'LL BUY, WHO'LL BUY
THE BOOKS OF A BUSTED BIBLIOPHILE?

And in imagination I can hear the auctioneer saying :
"Now, ladies and gentlemen, if I may have your
attention, we will sell the library of a collector well
known to many of you. The books are all in good
condition, having been collected by one who was
careful to admit nothing into his library, etc. If you
will turn to the first item in your catalogue, we'll
begin the sale. 'A'Beckett, Comic History of England. First edition, two volumes, in original cloth.'
How much am I bid? — Thank you," and so on,
down to Zaehnsdorf's "Short History of Book-
binding."

And it won't be so bad ! Better men than I have
parted with their books — better men, mind you,
but none with a greater love of books than I ; and
if my present collection has to be jettisoned, I'll at
once begin collecting over again. Not from me shall
arise a sombre sonnet, "To My Books on Parting
With Them"—for two reasons : in the first place,
I could not write a sonnet with a set of the "first
folios" as a reward ; and the second reason is temperamental : I have never allowed myself to become
"sicklied o'er with the pale cast of thought."

And maybe the sale won't take place, after all.

Maybe I'll be able to compound with my creditors for a penny in the pound. I have heard of such terms, and I cannot imagine anything more satisfactory. I must have had some such terms as these in my mind when a little Skelton worked its way into my library, and took its place on my shelves just alongside my copy of the first edition of Piers Plowman. Now, Skeltons are rare; even Beverly Chew admits that. What was it he said in his introduction to the sale catalogue of the Hagen books? "If I were asked what is the scarcest item in the sale, I should unhesitatingly say, that charming little volume containing four poems of John Skelton, Poet Laureate to King Henry VII." That little paragraph did for me, followed as it was by this: "One who followed with some apprehension Mr. Hagen's continual investment in books said he thought he would do better to purchase good bonds. 'No,' said Hagen, 'my books are worth more than your bonds.' Let

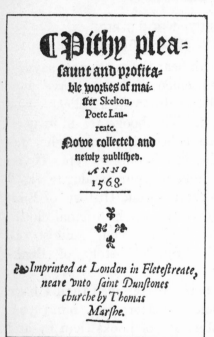

Pithy plea=
saunt and profita=
ble workes of mai=
ster Skelton,
Poete Lau-
reate.
Nowe collected and
newly publifhed.
ANNO
1568.

Imprinted at London in Fleteftreate,
neare vnto faint Dunftones
churche by Thomas
Marfhe.

us hope he was right; recent events would seem to confirm his judgment."

Well, it turned out just as he had hoped. I went to the sale with that "What would the Vanderbilts buy?" story in the back of my head; and from where I sat it seemed as if the whole family were competing for the Skelton. I don't know who got it, but the auctioneer's hammer fell when someone said "$9700," and then and there I determined to have a Skelton—not the edition of 1520, of course, but a Skelton, nevertheless: say the "Pithy, Pleasaunt and Profitable Workes, nowe collected and newly published. Anno 1568." And so

(Observe the spelling of the author's name in this facsimile.)

when, a year or two later, a fine black-letter copy in contemporary vellum turned up in London, where Wells got it and brought it to New York, what was I to do? Reader, what would you have done? Well, that's exactly what I did, and that's how this dainty little volume snuggled its way into this room, where it seemingly is quite as much at home as it was in Mr. Thomas Marshe's shoppe in Fletestreate neare unto saint Dunstones Churche, three hundred and fifty years ago. I smoked several cheap cigars on the night of its arrival — one has to economize in something.

One great temptation I have so far avoided,— Restoration Plays,— assisted in my escape by their rarity and consequent high prices. These little volumes, many of them bearing titles which can hardly be mentioned when ladies are around, fascinate scholar and collector alike. No one who knows him would, I fancy, dispute Dr. Schelling's claim to have read every old play in our literature. And they had the same fascination for Trollope, who in his "Autobiography" says : "Of late years, putting aside the Latin classics, I have found my greatest pleasure in our old English dramatists,— not from any excessive love of their work, which often irritates me by its want of truth to nature even while it shames me by its language,— but from curiosity in searching their plots and examining their character. If I live a few years longer, I shall, I think, leave in my copies of these dramatists, down to the close of James I, written criticisms on every play. No one who has not looked closely into it knows how many there are.

But if I have so far withstood the lure of the drama, the desire to own first editions of those poets who have done so much to fix our language and who have enriched our common inheritance beyond that of other nations, is strong and will not be denied. Although I boast a "Colin Clout" and "The Faerie Queene," it is not until I reach the "Hesperides" of

Herrick that I really enjoy myself. This lovely book
opens up a whole train of wants, satisfied, thank
Heaven, in Lovelace's "Lucasta," Suckling's "Frag-
menta Aurea," and Carew (one of the Gentlemen of
the Privie Bed-Chamber and Sewer in Ordinary to
His Majesty), his "Po-
ems," and many more,
right down to Brown-
ing's "Men and Wom-
en," two small volumes,
containing some of his
best poetry, without
which no collection of
the poets is worthy of
the name.

It is a curious thing,
what trifling incidents
give a slant to one's collecting; all through life
it is the same story
One goes to a party,
passes a dish of ice-
cream to a person with
a pair of particularly bright eyes, becomes engaged,
married, and done for almost before one knows it.
My interest in Defoe came about just as fortuitously.
Many years ago I was spending a week or so in Oxford, occasionally running up to London on business.
One day my affairs took me into the City Road, and
having an hour to spare, I spent it prowling around
in Bunhill Fields Burying Ground, looking at the

graves of the all-but-forgotten worthies buried there.
Quite unexpectedly I came upon the grave of Bunyan, and a little later upon that of Defoe, erected by
the subscriptions of
the school-children
of England. The dis-
covery gave me a
pleasant thrill. That
evening, after dinner,
in a tiny smoking-
room of the King's
Arms in Oxford, I
fell into conversation
with an American
gentleman who ap-
peared interested in
Defoe, and to him,
in a few well-chosen
words, I imparted my
opinion of the author
of "Robinson Cru-
soe." He agreed with
me, set me right here

POEMS.

By
THOMAS CAREW
Efquire.

One of the Gentlemen of the
Privie-Chamber, and Sewer in
Ordinary to His Majefty.

_____

_____

LONDON,
Printed by *I. D.* for *Thomas Walkley,*
and are to be fold at the figne of the
flying Horfe, between Brittains
Burfe, and York-Houfe.
1640

and there, and was a very charming companion altogether. Subsequently, I was rather disconcerted when
I discovered that I had been explaining Defoe to the
greatest living authority on that author — Professor
William P. Trent of Columbia University. He was
spending a summer in Oxford, engaged in the well-
nigh insuperable task of studying Defoe pamphlets
in the Bodleian Library.

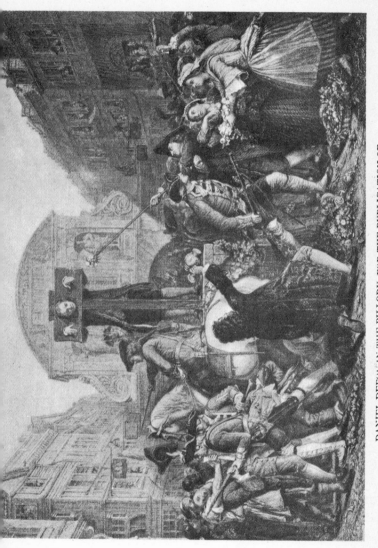

DANIEL DEFOE IN THE PILLORY, FOR THE PUBLICATION OF
"THE SHORTEST WAY WITH DISSENTERS"

Here, just before Temple Bar, he received the plaudits of the crowd

As a child, I think I preferred "The Swiss Family Robinson" to "Robinson Crusoe," and I remember wondering what relation the one Robinson was to the other. We are told that the discovery of the print of a man's naked foot in the sand is the greatest bit of realism in fiction. No doubt it is, but we must not overlook the "Journal of the Plague Year." It was published shortly after "Robinson Crusoe"; and of the many books on the Great Plague of London, it is the only one that has survived "the tooth of envious time." It remained for another American scholar, Dr. Watson Nicholson, to point out the manner in which this book was compiled. Defoe, sometimes called the father of the English novel, was in fact what we would to-day call a journalist. He set himself to a piece of work, got his facts together as accurately as he could, working under pressure,— writing, so to speak, against time,— and then, by representing him-

A

JOURNAL

OF THE

Plague Year:

BEING

Obfervations or Memorials,

Of the moft Remarkable

OCCURRENCES,

As well

PUBLICK *as* PRIVATE,

Which happened in

L O N D O N

During the laft

GREAT VISITATION
In 1665.

Written by a CITIZEN who continued all the while in *London.* Never made publick before

L O N D O N:

Printed for *E. Nutt* at the *Royal-Exchange*; *J. Roberts* in *Warwick-Lane*; *A. Dodd* without *Temple-Bar*; and *J. Graves* in St. *James's-ftreet.* 1722.

self as present at the events which he describes, deceived his readers so completely that they accepted the result as the actual narration of an eye-witness. First of all regarded as an authentic history, next as clever fiction, we to-day know the book for what it is: a hastily written but wonderfully realistic account of one of the most tragic events in the history of the city of London. Throughout its entire length, every page records some fact or fancy which makes for reality. My copy is in superlative condition—bound but uncut, as is also my "Moll Flanders," with its all-comprehending title-page. And there are many more.

THE

FORTUNES

AND

MISFORTUNES

Of the FAMOUS

Moll Flanders, &c.

Who was Born in NEWGATE, and during a Life of continu'd Variety for Threescore Years, befides her Childhood, was Twelve Year a *Whore*, five times a *Wife* (whereof once to her own Brother) Twelve Year a *Thief*, Eight Year a Tranfported *Felon* in *Virginia*, at laft grew *Rich*, liv'd *Honeft*, and died a *Penitent*,

Written from her own MEMORANDUMS.

LONDON: Printed for, and Sold by W, CHETWOOD, at *Cato's-Head*, in *Ruffel-ftreet, Covent-Garden*; and T. EDLING, at the *Prince's-Arms*, over-againft *Exerter-Change* in the *Strand*. MDDCXXI.

It is only a step from Defoe to Samuel Pepys. There is one book, at least, which no reader, be he judicious or she gentle, will wish to have in first edition — the immortal "Diary." On three separate occasions did I journey from London to Cambridge to see the Pepysian Library, each time to be told that the custodian "regretted that it was impossible." If my visit fell on a Tuesday, it was on a Wednesday that the library could be seen; if I called in the morning, the afternoon was the proper time. Once I tried "the silver key," but was unsuccessful; perhaps it was not large enough. The last time I was in Cambridge, however, I was fortunate enough one day, in Mr. Heffer's bookshop, to be introduced to the present librarian or custodian, Mr. O. F. Morshead, and I had the great pleasure of spending a morning in the library under his delightful guidance, looking at such treasures as would cause the heart of the coldest book-collector — and I am not the coldest — to throb with excitement.

Pepys began his diary when he was twenty-seven years of age. He gave up keeping it, on account of failing eyesight, when he was but thirty-six, which, he says, was "almost as much as to see myself go into my grave." But he remained a collector all his life, and he did not die until he was past seventy. Not until after the close of the Diary did he reach the maturity of his power in the Navy.

What treasures can a rich and industrious man accumulate in forty years! Particularly if, as was at least once the case, he borrowed and did not return. One item he obtained in this way from his brother diarist, John Evelyn. It is a pocket-book, a sort of an almanac, formerly the property of his great hero, Francis Drake, with his name, spelled "Drak," written therein. It is of course of supreme interest, and Pepys, who numbered all his books, gave it number 1.

Pepys's books, about three thousand in all, repose

in the original bookcases which he had made in 1666 by Mr. Sympson, "the joyner." They are arranged according to a curious scheme of his own, exactly as he left them. In point of fact, the shorthand manuscript of the Diary is, at a cursory glance, one of the least interesting things in the collection. But what a story is locked up in the six volumes of closely written cypher!

Under the terms of Pepys's will, Magdalene College is intrusted with the care of the collection, with reversion to Trinity in the event that there is any default in the rules and regulations laid down by Pepys for its safe keeping; and the manuscript of the Diary slumbered among Pepys's books from his death in 1703 to 1825, when it was deciphered and published. But in the first edition, only about half of the Diary was published, and this was edited and expurgated by Lord Braybrooke to an extent which became apparent only by degrees. Some years later, a clergyman took the matter in hand and, omitting what seemed good to him, suggested that the complete work might be found "tedious"! Finally, and not until 1893, there appeared an edition, edited by H. B. Wheatley, which gave the Diary complete, with the exception of a few passages, amounting in all to about one page of text, which, he says, cannot possibly be printed.

What a book it is! Without style, or wit, or eloquence; but for what book having all these qualities would we exchange it? As someone has said, Rousseau is positively secretive in comparison with Pepys.

THE BUILDING THAT HOUSES THE PEPYSIAN LIBRARY IN CAMBRIDGE

The charm of the Diary is its quaint and utter shame-
lessness, as when its author confesses that he kick 1
one of his maids and is not sorry for it, but he is
sorry that he was seen doing so. Most of us are more
like Pepys than we would be willing to confess. We
do wrong and carry our heads high, and are ashamed
only when we are
found out.

And now I find my-
self wondering wheth-
er I have written all
this just to intro-
duce a charming bal-
lade, worthy of Austin
Dobson at his best, by
my friend "Kit" Mor-
ley, or as a pretext for
referring to my beau-
tiful copy of Pepys's
Memoires of the Roy-
al Navy. Let me give
the ballade first.

It would seem from
an entry in the Diary under date of February 3, 1665,
that Pepys had taken a vow to abstain from kissing
pretty women and, in the event of his breaking it,
to give to some good cause a shilling for each kiss
after the first one. He was a methodical scamp, but
I doubt if he could accurately keep count. In any
event, on this day, in addition to Mrs. Turner having
shown him something that he ardently admires, he

THE EIGHTH SIN

BY

C. D. MORLEY

"There is no greater Sin after the seven deadly
than to flatter oneself into an idea of being a great
Poet." *Letters of John Keats.*

OXFORD
B. H. BLACKWELL, BROAD STREET
LONDON
SIMPKIN, MARSHALL & CO. LIMITED
MCMXII

records meeting, "among the others, pretty Mrs. Margaret who indeed is a very pretty lady; and, though by my vow it costs me 12*d*. a kiss, yet I did venture upon a couple."

Good Mr. Peeps or Peps or Pips
    (However he should be yclept),
Clerk of the King's Bureau of Ships,
    A very spicy journal kept.
He knew a lemon from a peach,
    And, among other things, he knew,
When kisses are a shilling each,
    We should adventure on a few!

He was a connoisseur of lips,
    And though I cannot quite accept
Some of his rather shady tips
    (I grant he often overstepped
The bounds of taste) — still he can teach
    Misogynists a thing or two —
When kisses are a shilling each,
    We should adventure on a few!

He drank the wine of life by sips,
    He roundly ate and soundly slept,
His spirits suffered no eclipse,
    But Lord! how sore he would have wept
To see his private linen bleach
    And flutter in the public view —
Well, kisses are a shilling each;
    Let us adventure on a few!

ENVOY

O Ballad-monger, I beseech,
    Consider his advice anew;
When kisses are a shilling each,
    Why not adventure on a few?

MAP OF ENGLAND, EVERY LINE OF WHICH IS EMBROIDERED
IN COLORED SILK

The making of these maps antedated the "movies" by a century or more

This clever poem first appeared in a little paper-backed volume of verse, "The Eighth Sin," published by Blackwell in Oxford in 1912, when Morley, one of three brothers, all Rhodes scholars, was an undergraduate. It is much sought by collectors, and gets its title from a sentence in one of Keats's letters, "There is no greater Sin after the seven deadly than to flatter oneself into an idea of being a great Poet." And with this sentiment I am in full accord.

The "Memoires Relating to the State of the Royal Navy of England" is a scarce book, with a fine portrait of Pepys after

Memoires

Relating to the

S T A T E

OF THE

ROYAL NAVY

O F

E N G L A N D,

For Ten Years, Determin'd
December 1688.

By Samuel Pepys

*Quantis moleſtiis vacant, qui nihil omninò
cum Populo contrahunt? Quid Dulcius
Otio Litterato?* Cic. Tuſc. Diſp.

L O N D O N:

Printed for *Ben. Griffin,* and are to be ſold
by *Sam. Keble* at the Great *Turks-Head* in
Fleet-ſtreet over againſt *Fetter-Lane,* 1690.

Kneller, and, to be correct, must have a large folded plate giving an account of the finances of the Navy with the Exchequer. This plate, as the catalogues say, is "frequently lacking." I had almost forgotten that I have, too, a fine letter from Pepys to his nephew and heir, John Jackson, bidding him, when he buys anything such as books, or prints, to "get very good ones only"; excellent advice for the collector, and too little considered in Pepys's time.

There are, it is said, seventeen ways of spelling the Diarist's name, but only three of pronouncing it; which is correct, is still a vexed question. Let me quote a little verse by Ashby Sterry, which all the papers were copying twenty-five years or so ago, and which found its way into my scrap-book.

There are people, I'm told — some say there are heaps —
Who speak of the talkative Samuel as Peeps;
And some so precise and pedantic their step is,
Who call the delightful old diarist Pepys;
But those I think right, and I follow their steps,
Ever mention the garrulous gossip as Peps.

"And so to bed."

IV

WHAT IS THE MATTER WITH THE BOOKSHOP?

SOME time ago my friend Mr. William Harris Arnold told me that he had written a paper on the welfare of the bookstore. When it appeared in the "Atlantic Monthly," I read it attentively, and I disagree with his conclusions. As it seems to me that the subject is one in which all who read should be interested, I should like to present my views for what they may be worth.

Mr. Arnold's remedy for the situation, admittedly difficult, in which the retail booksellers find themselves is to have publishers grant to booksellers "the option of taking books by outright purchase or on memorandum" — that is to say, on sale, and subject to return. I remember once, years ago, hearing the late Andrew Carnegie say to a body of business men that, if he were in a business in which it was impossible for him to tell, at least approximately, how much money he had made or lost in a given month, he would get out of that business. He said that the next best thing to making money was to know that you were not making it — and apply the remedy. Now, if a publisher should establish in any large way the custom of disposing of his publications "on sale," as the phrase is, I should like to know when, if ever, he could go before his creditors, represented by authors, printers, paper-makers, and binders, and declare himself solvent and worthy of their further confidence.

It seems to me that publishers assume sufficient risk, as it is. Many books, I fancy, just about pay their way, showing very little of either profit or loss; there may be a small profit resulting from the average book, and the exceptional book shows either a handsome profit — or a large loss. "The Four Horsemen of the Apocalypse," is the most recent of great successes : edition followed edition in such quick succession that the publishing facilities of New York City were heavily drawn upon to keep up with the demand. On the other hand, many years ago, the publication of "Endymion," by Disraeli, then Earl of Beaconsfield, occasioned an enormous loss. His publishers brought out this novel in the then customary three-volume form for, I think, two guineas. No one read into the middle of the second volume. It was a complete failure. A few months after publication every second-hand bookshop in London was trying to dispose of uncut, and unopened, "library" copies at about the cost of binding. It must be admitted that these are extreme instances : the profit in the one case must have amounted to a small fortune ; the losses in the other might have driven the publisher into bankruptcy.

The publishing business has always been regarded as extra-hazardous — more respectable than the theatrical business and less exciting, but resembling it in that one never knows whether one is embarked

FOUR DISTINGUISHED COLLECTORS

PROF. C. B. TINKER   MR. W. H. ARNOLD
MR. R. B. ADAM   MR. W. F. GABLE

upon a success or a failure until it is too late to withdraw. And it has always been so. Sir Walter Scott,
whose career as a publisher is not always remembered,
said that the booksellers, as publishers were called in
his day, were "the only tradesmen in the world who
professedly and by choice dealt in what is called 'a
pig in a poke,' publishing twenty books in hopes of
hitting upon one good speculation, as a person buys
shares in a lottery in hopes of gaining a prize"; and
Sir Walter had reason to know, as had also Mark
Twain.

I remember that, some years ago, a little book,
"A Publisher's Confessions," was issued anonymously
by Doubleday, Page & Co. It recited the difficulties,
financial and other, of a firm of publishers, and is now
generally understood to have been written by Walter
Hines Page, our late Ambassador to the Court of St.
James's. The writer's conclusion was that men of
such distinction as those who control the organiza-
tions known as Scribners, Macmillans, and others of
like standing, could earn very much more by devot-
ing their abilities to banking, railroads, or other lines
of business; for, he said, "publishing as publishing
is the least profitable of all professions, except
preaching and teaching, to each of which it is a sort
of cousin." And it is to this harassed person, per-
plexed, by reason of the nature of his calling, beyond
most business men, that Mr. Arnold would add the
financing of the countless bookstores, in many cases
in incompetent hands, all over the country, from
Maine to California. His suggestion is interesting,

but I doubt if publishers in any large numbers will take kindly to it. They will probably feel that Mr. Arnold, whom I last saw in his own library surrounded by his own priceless books, apparently free from problems of any kind, has suggested a remedy worse than the disease from which they are suffering.

It is, however, to the bookseller rather than to the publisher that my heart goes out. The publishers of the present day, at least those I know, ride around in limousine cars while the booksellers walk — the floor. When Hogg threatened to knock the brains out of a bookseller, Sir Walter Scott cried, "Knock the brains into him, my dear Hogg, but for God's sake don't knock any out." The difficulties from which he is chiefly suffering are two : first, the unfair competition of certain department stores, and second, that we, the readers, have deserted him. A rich, intelligent, and extravagant people, we know nothing, and seemingly wish to know nothing, of the pleasure of buying and owning books. As I see it, the decay of the bookshop set in years ago with the downfall of the lyceum, the debating society, and the lecture platform. We have none of these things now, and if we had not largely given up reading as one of the consequences, I should not be sorry ; but the mental stimulation that comes from personal contact has been lost, and seemingly there is nothing that will take its place. Of course, when I say that we have none of these things, I mean in proportion to our population and wealth.

When it comes to book-buying, we seem so loath

to take a chance. We pay four or six or ten dollars
for a pair of tickets for a "show,"— how I hate the
word ! — sit through it for an entire evening, and
when asked what we thought of it, answer briefly,
"Rotten," and dismiss the matter from our minds.
Now book-buying is, or ought to be, a pleasure. If
one comes in contact with a fairly well-informed sales-
man or saleswoman, it may be a delight. And there
are such. To speak of those I know, if you care for
illustrated or extra-illustrated books, where can you
find a more interesting character than George Rigby
in Philadelphia ? And there is Mabel Zahn, at
Sessler's — "Dere Mable," as I sometimes call her :
many a time she has shamed me with her knowledge.
And there is Leary's, one of the largest and best
second-hand bookshops in the country ; you are not
importuned to buy, you may browse there by the
hour. We in Philadelphia hold its proprietor in such
esteem that we made him mayor of our city, and
finally governor of our state. He has known me ever
since I was a little boy, and it was a proud day for
me when I thought I could safely refer to him as my
friend Ned Stuart.

Leary's is one of the few bookshops in which bar-
gains may still be found. My friend Tinker — dear
old Tink — never comes to Philadelphia without
spending a few hours at Leary's ; and only yesterday
James Shields, that astute bookman, dropping in
upon me to ask a question, which, naturally, I was
unable to answer, showed me a ten-dollar bill he had
just extracted from Lawler, Rosenbach's manager, for

a book he had just "picked up" at Leary's for fifty cents. These things can still be done, but it takes more exact knowledge than I have been able to acquire. One thing yet remains to be told : the price at which Lawler sold the book. Who knows ?

In an effort to escape the blame that should be ours, we sometimes say that Mr. Andrew Carnegie, who scattered public libraries all over the land in an effort, relatively successful, to die poor, is responsible for the plight in which the booksellers find themselves; but I am willing to acquit the libraries of all blame. They do an immense amount of good. I never go to a strange city without visiting its library, and I count many librarians among my friends; but I am, nevertheless, always overwhelmed in the presence of countless thousands of books, as I might be in the presence of crowned heads; indeed, I think that, idle curiosity once gratified, crowned heads would not impress me at all.

And so it is that, not being a scholar, or altogether indigent, I do not much use any library except my own. I early formed the habit of buying books, and, thank God, I have never lost it. Authors living and dead — dead, for the most part — afford me my greatest enjoyment, and it is my pleasure to buy more books than I can read. Who was it who said, "I hold the buying of more books than one can peradventure read, as nothing less than the soul's reaching towards infinity; which is the only thing that raises us above the beasts that perish"? Whoever it was, I agree with him; and the same idea has been less sententiously expressed by Ralph Bergengren in that charming little poem in "Jane, Joseph and John," the loveliest book for children and grown-ups since R. L. S. gave us his "Child's Garden of Verses."

My Pop is always buying books:
So that Mom says his study looks
Just like an old bookstore.
The bookshelves are so full and tall,
They hide the paper on the wall,
   And there are books just everywhere,
   On table, window-seat, and chair,
And books right on the floor.

And every little while he buys
More books, and brings them home and tries
To find a place where they will fit,
And has an awful time of it.

Once, when I asked him why he got
So many books, he said, "Why not?"
I've puzzled over that a lot,

Too many of us, who are liberal, not to say lavish, in our household expenses, seem to regard the purchase of books as an almost not-to-be-permitted extravagance. We buy piano-players and talking machines, and we mortgage our houses to get an automobile, but when it comes to a book, we exhaust every resource before parting with our money. If we cannot borrow a book from a friend, we borrow it from a library; if there is anything I like less than lending a book, it is borrowing one, and I know no greater bore than the man who insists on lending you a book which you do not intend to read. Of course,

you can cure him, ultimately, by losing the volume;
but the process takes time.

My philosophy of life is very simple; one does n't
have to study the accursed German philosophers —
or any other — to dis-
cover that the way to
happiness is to get a
day's pleasure every
day,— I am not writ-
ing as a preacher,—
and I know no greater
pleasure than taking
home a bundle of
books which you have
deprived yourself of
something, to buy.

"I never buy new
books," a man once
said to me, looking at
a pile on my library
table; "I 've got
to economize some-
where, and they are so expensive."

"And yet," I retorted, "you enjoy reading; don't
you feel under any obligation to the authors from
whom you derive so much pleasure? Someone has
to support them. I confess to the obligation."

When I think how much pleasure I get from reading, I feel it my duty to buy as many current books
as I can. I "collect" Meredith and Stevenson, the
purchase of whose books no longer benefits them.

ABRAHAM LINCOLN

A Play
By John Drinkwater

*For
W. T.... A Edward Newton
with every good wish from
John Drinkwater*

*November 11ᵗʰ 1920
London*

*When the high heart we magnify,
And the sure vision celebrate,
And worship greatness passing by,
Ourselves are great.*

London: Sidgwick & Jackson, Ltd.
3 Adam Street, Adelphi. MCMXVIII

Why should I not also collect George Moore or Locke or Conrad or Hergesheimer ? which, by the way, I do. And while you may not be able to get such an inscription in your copy of the first edition of Drinkwater's "Abraham Lincoln" as I have in mine, you should get a copy of the book before it is too late. All these men are engaged in carrying on the glorious tradition of English literature. It is my duty to give them what encouragement I can ; to pay tribute to them. I wish I were not singular in this.

But to return to the bookshop. In addition to having to compete with the many forms of amusement unknown fifty years ago,— it would be superfluous for me to do more than mention the latest of them, the "movie," — the bookshop elects to sell a "nationally advertised" article in competition with the department store. The publishers allow what would be a fairly liberal margin of profit, if the bookshops were permitted to keep it ; but the department stores cut that margin to the quick. For reasons that are well known, it is profitable for them to do so : with their immense "turnover" and their relatively small "overhead," they can afford to sell certain popular books at cut prices, for the reason that at the next counter they are selling chocolates, marked "WEEK-END SPECIAL, 70c. *Regular Price* $1.00," which do not cost over forty cents, perhaps less ; and often they do get a dollar for these boxes. And what is true of chocolates is true of practically everything they sell, except books and a few other specialties, which they use as "leaders."

Books are the only "nationally advertised" specialties that anyone pretends to sell in shops almost exclusively devoted to them.   Time was, and it was a sad time, when the monthly magazines, "Atlantic," "Harper's," "Scribner's," and the rest, which cost $28 per hundred, wholesale, were retailed in a large store in Philadelphia for 25 cents each. The highest court to which the question can be carried has ruled that the seller can sell at any price he pleases, provided that he does not misstate the facts, as, for example, that his immense purchasing power enables him to undersell his competitors. In some few cases the publishers provide "specials," too: they give extra discounts for quantities; and there are always, alas, "remainders," sold at a loss by the publishers and at quite a tidy little profit by the retailer; but in general the facts are as I have stated.

It must be admitted that the department store helps the publisher by selling hundreds of thousands of copies of books like "Dere Mable" and the "Four Horsemen." "The Young Visiters," too, whether it be by Barrie or another, sold enormously; but just so large as is the sale of books like these, just so small is the sale of books of enduring merit. Perhaps I am wrong, but I fancy that men prefer to buy what I may call good books, while women buy novels and the lighter forms of literature.

Now, fancy a man going into a certain department store that I have in mind, and asking for a copy of "Tom Jones." He is met by a young lady in a low-cut dress, standing in high-heeled slippers, with her

hair gathered up in large puffs which entirely conceal
her ears; her nose has been recently powdered, and
she looks as if she might be going to a party. "Tom
Jones!" she says; "is it a boy's book? Juveniles,
second to the right." "No, it's a novel," you say;
and she replies, "Fiction, second to the left."

You move on, avoiding a table on which is a sign,
"The Newest Books Are On This Table," and you
meet another young lady, also ready for a party,
and repeat your question. "Is it a new book?" she
says. "No," you explain; and she conducts you to a
case containing hundreds of volumes of the Every-
man's Series — and an excellent series it is. But the
books have been skillfully shuffled, and what you
seek is hard to find. While you and she are looking,
someone "cuts in" and inquires for a copy of "Java
Head," to which she promptly replies, "One sixty-
nine," and conducts her customer to a large pile,
behind which she disappears and is seen, by you, no
more.

You keep on looking until someone comes to your
rescue, and asks if she can do anything for you. You
say "'Tom Jones,'" and she, being an intelligent
person, says, "Fielding," and conducts you to the
fine-book department, where you are finally shown
a set of Fielding flashily bound in what appears to be
morocco, marked $40. You demur at the price and
explain that you want "Tom Jones" to read, not a
set to put upon your shelves; finally, thanking the
"saleslady" for her trouble, you go out empty-
handed, having wasted half an hour.

If this paper should be read by the proprietor of a retail store, or by his intelligent clerk, I can hear him cry, "You are quite right, but we know all this. Have you any remedy?" Certainly I have nothing to suggest which will prove a royal road to fortune; but I do suggest the selling of good second-hand books along with current publications, and I would stress the second-hand, and call it the rare-book department, for the profits of that department will be found to be surprisingly large. I would say to the proprietor of the bookshop, "Bring some imagination to bear on your business." Imagination is as necessary to a successful tradesman as to the poet. He is, indeed, only a day-laborer without it. I am reminded of one of the clever bits in Pinero's play, "Iris." A tall distinguished-looking man enters; his appearance instantly challenges attention, and the *ingénue* inquires who he is, and is told, "That is Mr. Maldonadno, the great financier." Then comes the question, "What is a financier?" and the telling reply, "A financier, my dear, is a pawnbroker — with imagination."

The point is well made. What quality was it in Charles M. Schwab which, while most of the great business men in America were wringing their hands over what appeared to be their impending ruin, when the war broke out, sent him off to England, to return quickly with hundreds of millions of dollars' worth of orders in his pocket? Imagination! It was this same quality, working in conjunction with the imagination of the late J. P. Morgan, which led to the formation of the great Steel Corporation.

There may be little room for the display of this supreme qualification in the retail book-business, but there is room for some. Be enterprising. Get good people about you. Make your shop-windows and your shops attractive. The fact that so many young men and women enter the teaching profession shows that there are still some people willing to scrape along on comparatively little money for the pleasure of following an occupation in which they delight. It is as true to-day as it was in Chaucer's time that there is a class of men who "gladly learn and gladly teach," and our college trustees and overseers and rich alumni take advantage of this, and expect them to live on wages which an expert chauffeur would regard as insufficient. Any bookshop worthy of survival can offer inducements at least as great as the average school or college. Under pleasant conditions you will meet pleasant people, for the most part, whom you can teach and from whom you may learn something. We used to hear much of the elevation of the stage; apparently that has been given over; let us elevate the bookshop. It can be done. My friend, Christopher Morley,—

> . . . Phœbus! what a name
> To fill the speaking-trump of future fame! —

in his delightful "Parnassus on Wheels," shows that there may be plenty of "uplift" and a world of romance in a traveling man well stocked with books. Indeed, a pleasant holiday could be planned along the lines of Roger Mifflin's novel venture in bookselling. I prophesy for this book, some day, such fame as is now enjoyed by Stevenson's "Travels with a Donkey." It is, in fact, just such a book, although admittedly the plump white horse, Pegasus, lacks somewhat the temperamental charm of R. L. S.'s best-drawn female character, Modestine.

I was in a college town recently, and passing a shop, I noticed some books in the window and at once entered, as is my habit, to look around. But I stayed only a moment, for in the rear of the shop I saw a large sign reading, "Laundry Received before 9 A.M. Returned the Same Day" — enterprise, without a doubt, but misdirected. If the bookshop is to survive, it must be made more attractive. The buying of books must be made a pleasure, just as the reading of them is; so that an intellectual man or woman with a leisure hour may spend it pleasantly and profitably increasing his or her store.

Every college town should support a bookshop. It need not necessarily be so splendid an undertaking as the Brick Row Print and Book Shop at New Haven, over which Byrne Hackett presides with such distinction, or even the Dunster House Book-Shop of Mr. Firuski of Cambridge. And to make these ventures the successes they deserve to be, faculty and students and the public alike should be loyal customers; but it should be remembered that these shops need not, and do not, depend entirely upon local trade. Inexpensive little catalogues can be issued and sent to customers half-way round the world.

CHRISTOPHER MORLEY

Whose graceful verses and charming essays are known to all who love books; for whose first volume,
"*Parnassus on Wheels,*" *I have prophesied such fame as is now enjoyed by R. L S.'s*
"*Travels with a Donkey*"

Speaking of catalogues, I have just received one from a shop I visited when I was last in London, called " The Serendipity Shop." It is located in a little slum known as Shepherd's Market, right in the heart of Mayfair. It may be that my readers will be curious to know how it gets its name. "Serendipity" was coined by Horace Walpole from an old name for Ceylon — Serendip. He made it, as he writes his friend Mann, out of an old fairy tale wherein the heroes "were always making discoveries, by accidents and sagacity, of things they were not in quest of." Its name, therefore, suggests that, although you may not find in the Serendipity Shop what you came for, you will find something that you want, although you did not know it when you came in. Its proprietor, Mr. Everard Meynell, is the son of Alice Meynell, who, with her husband, did so much to relieve the sufferings of that fine poet, Francis Thompson, and who is herself a poet and essayist of distinction. Is not every bookshop in fact, if not in name, a Serendipity Shop?

I have no patience with people who affect to be fond of reading, and who seem to glory in their ignorance of editions. "All I am interested in," they say, "is the type: so long as the type is readable, I care for nothing else." This is a rather common form of cant. Everything about a book should be as sound and honest and good; but it need not be expensive.

I have always resented William Morris's attitude toward books. Constantly preaching on art and beauty for the people, he set about producing books which are as expensive as they are beautiful, which only rich men can buy, and which not one man in a hundred owning them reads. Whereas my friend Mr. Mosher of Portland, Maine,— I call him friend because we have tastes in common; I have, in point of fact, never met him or done more than exchange a check for a book with him,— has produced, not a few, but hundreds of books which are as nearly fault-less as books can be, at prices which are positively cheap. As is well known, Mr. Mosher relies very little upon the bookshops for the marketing of his product, but sells practically his entire output to individual buyers, by means of catalogues which are works of art in themselves. We may not fully real-ize it, but when Mr. Mosher passes away, booklovers of another generation will marvel at the certitude of his taste, editorial and other; for he comes as near to being the ideal manufacturer as any man who ever lived.

I would not for a moment contend that a man in the retail book-business will in a short time make a for-tune. We are not a nation of readers, but a young and uncultured people. It is not to be forgotten, however, that we graduate every year an immense number of men and women from our colleges. Poten-tially, these are, or ought to be, readers; they will be readers, if publishers and booksellers do their duty.

If a library is the best university, as we have been told it is, the bookseller has his cue. Let him make his shop attractive — a centre from which culture may be radiated.   Customers have to be educated. When a new line of goods, of whatever kind, is being introduced, "missionary work," as we manufacturers call it, has to be done.

New York City has several fine bookshops : for example, Brentano's, one of the great bookshops of the world ; but Brentano's has its fine-book department, as have Scribner's and Dutton's and Putnam's ; and these so-called fine-book departments are doing expensively, as befits New York, what I would have every bookshop do according to its *locale,* as McClurg is doing in Chicago.

The advantages that would accrue are several. More readers would be made.   The book-business of the department stores would not be interfered with in the least — they would remain, as now, the best customers for certain classes of publishers, who might expect to have some day, in addition, a more thriving class of booksellers than now.   And better books would be published — better, that is, in print, paper, and binding.

In the fine-book department, which I am urging every bookseller to start without delay, I would keep out trash; I would admit only good books — good, I mean, in every sense of the word except moral. The department should be in charge of the most intelligent man in the shop, if there be an intelligent man ; and I would get one if I had not one, and in these days of profit-sharing, I would give him an interest in the profit of that department.   I would buy, too, good books from the second-hand English booksellers, who sell very cheaply; and above all things I would not forget the wisdom stored up in the distorted proverb,—

> Early to bed and early to rise,
> Work like h—— , and advertise.

V

A SLOGAN FOR BOOKSELLERS

I don't think that I was a very bad little boy, as boys go, but the fact is that I ran away from school — a boarding-school — and never went back. I did, however, apply for a job in a bookstore, got the promise of the next vacancy, and sat down and waited. But not for long. Scanning the advertisements in the Philadelphia "Ledger," I discovered that a man was looking for me, and promptly decided that it was my duty to meet him half-way. "A bright, active boy to address envelopes. $3.00. Reference," was the way the advertisement read.

Thus it was that I first met Cyrus H. K. Curtis; not head on, not at right angles, but obliquely: we were both going in the same direction; he had not yet struck his gait, and for several months he did not appear to be leading me much; but gradually he increased the very considerable distance there was between us, and finally he passed out of sight. I did not see him again until he had become a national figure. He became this by advertising. Many men have made larger fortunes than he; with them advertising has been incidental, like love in a man's life; but with Mr. Curtis it has been his whole existence; and the largest and finest publishing building in the world is a monument to his skill as an advertiser.

There are people who affect to believe that advertising is economic waste; Mr. Curtis is not one of them. He has always taken his own medicine; he may believe in the Trinity; he may, for aught I know, repeat the Athanasian Creed on occasions; but I know, the whole world knows, that he is a believer in advertising; and he should be, for his success is due largely — not entirely, but largely — to it.

The Curtis Publishing Company, then, is admittedly the result of an advertising campaign, begun a long time ago, and carried on consistently day after day, month after month, year after year, with special reference to the product it has to sell, which is advertising. Incidentally it delivers something else,— several other things, to be exact,— and it delivers these at a cost to the "consumer" so trifling in proportion to the cost of production, that it almost amounts to a gift. I think I may say without fear of contradiction that the "Saturday Evening Post" is the cheapest piece of merchandise in the world. And if that be the case, what becomes of the theory of the economic waste of advertising?

But it is not the object of this paper to sing a hymn of praise, either to Mr. Curtis, or to his company, or to his product. I am interested chiefly in suggesting, if I may be permitted to do so, a campaign of advertising for publishers of another kind, namely, publishers of books. Books interest me enormously; they always have. They are the best of friends,— grave or gay as your humor is,— and you can shut them up when you want to. Most people don't care

for them much; they think they do, but they don't;
that is to say, they care for so many other things
more that, when it comes to buying them, they have
no money left. Now, next to a modicum of food and
a patch of clothes, I care more for books than for
anything else.

I should like to digress. I have reached the time
of life when Christmas means giving much and receiving little. I make no complaint, I only state the
fact. The table on which my presents are placed is
a very small one. The last present I received was
from my wife; it was a watch. I had a watch and
did not need another; but my wife thought I ought
to have a fine watch and she gave me one; and it was,
as I remember, about ten days after Christmas that,
in handing me a lot of household bills, she handed me
the bill for the watch, with the remark, "And you
might as well pay this, too; I thought I could, but it
would cramp me and you'll never know the difference." So with a sigh I bent my back to the burden,
and it was just as she had said.

A week later, going on a business trip somewhere,
I was sitting in a smoking-car, reading, when a man
whom I knew slightly asked me if I would not like
to sit into a friendly game of poker. I made known
to him briefly that I didn't know one card from another. Then, he said, "Let us talk," which meant,
let him talk; and talk he did, about everything and
nothing, until finally he asked me if I had received
any Christmas presents. This gave me a chance to
boast of my wife's generosity and to show my new

watch, with the result that my friend countered by saying that his wife had given him a fine antique bookcase.

"How very nice," I said. "Are you fond of books? Have you many?"

"No, not many," he replied; "but it is n't exactly a bookcase; it's more like a large upright writing-desk. The top is a closet, with glass doors with a red-silk lining; makes a nice place to keep whiskey and cigars and things under lock and key." (This was before we had discovered the necessity of keeping our whiskey in a burglar-proof vault.) "Then there's a flap that lets down on which you can write; and underneath is a place for books. And do you know," he continued, "*I know enough books already I'd like to have, to fill both shelves.*"

I shuddered, and the better to conceal my anguish I asked him if he enjoyed reading.

"Very much," he said; "I don't know anything I like better than to go into my den on Sunday morning after breakfast, and sit and read my newspaper undisturbed."

Think of a man staring vacantly at a Sunday paper, under the delusion that he is reading!

Now the fact is that many people, most people, have forgotten how to read, if they ever knew; and they have to be taught, and they can be taught, not only to read, but to buy books, by advertising. The use of tooth-powder has been enormously stimulated by advertising, and I am certain that a demand for books can be created in the same way, but it must be done wisely, systematically, and continuously. We are familiar with the proverb that "It is the first step that counts." Well, it is not so with advertising: in advertising, it is the last; the effect of advertising is cumulative. It is the last dollar spent that brings results. The first time one sees an advertisement, unless it is very striking, it has no pulling power; only after one has seen it repeatedly, does it begin to work.

The best advertising skill in the world was concentrated a year or two ago on Liberty Bonds. Most people did not know what a bond was; they had to be taught; and it is a thousand pities that, after people had been told that they were the finest investment in the world, they were allowed to decline so in price. We were told to "Buy and Borrow," and to "Buy till it hurts." Such is the effect of a forceful slogan a thousand times repeated, that we finally do as we are told. We bought and borrowed and got hurt, badly; I speak from experience.

Millions of people are seduced by the power of advertising to buy automobiles which they have no right to buy, because they are skillfully advertised and look so smart and so free from upkeep — in advertisements.

Advertising as an art or a science is essentially modern, in spite of the fact that Dr. Samuel Johnson, in one of his now little-read *Idlers*, written in 1759, refers to it as a "trade now so near to perfection that it is not easy to propose any improvement"; and he continues by saying, referring to the filling up of newspapers with advertisements: "The man who first took advantage of the general curiosity that was excited by a siege or battle, to betray the readers of news into the knowledge of the shop where the best puffs and powder were to be sold, was undoubtedly a man of great sagacity." It is our silly habit to think of Dr. Johnson, when we think of him at all, as ponderous and old-fashioned; ponderous he sometimes was, but he is quite up-to-date in calling advertisers "sagacious."

As I cannot suppose that my reader has at hand a newspaper containing such advertisements as called forth Dr. Johnson's encomiums, let me give a few examples taken almost at random from the "Daily Advertiser."

Mr. Pinchbeck, Senior, Clock and Watchmaker from Tunbridge Wells, having through a long series of repeated Injuries from his neighboring brother, Mr. Edward Pinchbeck, been obliged to alter his Sign, takes this method of informing the Public, that his, the said Pinchbeck senior's Sign is now only his late Father's Head, exactly opposite the Sun Tavern in Fleet Street.

Trouble was brewing, evidently, in the Pinchbeck family. "Thomas Madge, Watchmaker," was more fortunate: he announced that he was

Apprentice to the late Mr. Graham, and carries on the business in the same manner Mr. Graham did, at the Sign of the Dial opposite the Bolt and Tun in Fleet Street.

Dr. Johnson's *Dictionary* was proclaimed to the world in this fashion, the announcement occupying a space of a little more than an inch, single column: —

DR. JOHNSON, BY SIR JOSHUA REYNOLDS

From a photograph made by W. Vivian Chappel, from the original portrait, for this publication

This day is published in Two Volumes Folio Mr. S. Johnson's Dictionary of the English language. In which the words are deduced from their originals, and illustrated in their different significations by Examples from the Best Writers. To which are prefixed a History of the Language and an English Grammar. Printed for A. Millar.

And then follows the long list of booksellers financially interested in the venture.

As might be expected, "cures" for the diseases — real or imaginary—which plagued our forefathers occupied much space in the public prints, and of all the nostrums compounded by the apothecaries,— and their name is legion,— nothing was more advertised and consumed in greater quantities than Dr. James's Fever Powders. (Incidentally they killed Oliver Goldsmith, and Horace Walpole said he would take them if the house was on fire.) They were advertised as a "genuine medicine," and genuine medicines were prescribed by the pound or quart, as the apothecaries were not to be outdone in rigor by the surgeons, who "let blood" by the bucket at the

AN

ACCOUNT

OF THE LATE

Dr. GOLDSMITH's ILLNESS;

SO FAR AS RELATES TO THE

EXHIBITION

OF

Dr. JAMES's POWDERS:

TOGETHER WITH

REMARKS on the Use and Abuse of POWERFUL MEDICINES in the Beginning of FEVERS, and other ACUTE DISEASES.

By WILLIAM HAWES, APOTHECARY.

The THIRD EDITION; WITH CORRECTIONS, and an APPENDIX.

LONDON

Printed for W. BROWN, and H. GARDNER, in the Strand; J. HINTON, T. EVANS, and J. BEW, Paternoster-Row; S. HOOPER, Ludgate-Hill; J. WILLIAMS, Fleet-street; and W. DAVENHILL, opposite the Royal-Exchange. MDCCLXXIV.

[Price One Shilling.]

slightest provocation.   Prior to the introduction of
Dover's Powders and James's Powders, a man in a high
fever, if highly placed, might be considered to be worth
as much as sixty pounds to his apothecary.   Is it any
wonder, then, that well-advertised and fairly effica-
cious drugs, to be had for a few shillings, made fortunes
for their proprietors ?   All the more, since they were in
competition with such household remedies as "Syrup
of Snails," or a "broth" made of spiders ground fine
with opium in a mortar, and reduced to a liquid by
the addition of hot wine, to be drunk in bed, "covered
up warm and sweating."   What constitutions we
must have inherited from our ancestors, for only the
robust could have survived.

Such changes as have taken place in English newspaper advertising came slowly, and these have not
been to the advantage of the appearance of the newspaper.   A generation ago display advertising was
almost unknown.   Then, if a man wanted to occupy
the space of a column, say, he made a brief statement
and repeated it several, perhaps as many as a dozen,
times.   There was, and for aught I know, still may
be, a famous remedy, Beecham's Pills, with which
was coupled what we should to-day call a slogan,
"Worth a guinea a box."   No matter where one
turned, one read, "Beecham's Pills, Worth a guinea
a box"; or one could, if one preferred, read it, "Worth
a guinea a box, Beecham's Pills."   A fortune was
spent, and a larger fortune made, as one can still
make a fortune by advertising, if the article advertised has merit, as I presume Beecham's Pills had.

But steady; Mr. Beecham may by now be a knight or
a peer or something.   Yes, I have just looked him up
in "Who's Who." He is now "Sir Joseph Beecham,
Kt. cr. 1911; J. P., manufacturer and philanthropist,"
etc., etc.   Oh, yes, "It pays to advertise."

> Of that there is no manner of doubt —
> No possible, probable shadow of doubt —
> No possible doubt whatever,—

as the song in "The Gondoliers" goes.

To-day we are more sophisticated, and what our
advertising may become was very cleverly foretold
in a recent number of the "New Republic," in an
article in which it was suggested that a generation
hence every reference in reading matter will be made
to call attention to some article advertised.   If, for
example, a story of an elopement is to be told, the
hero, glancing at his watch (opposite the Elgin Watch
advertisement), will say that it is time to start.   "But
am I not to take my trunk?" (opposite the Inde-
structo Trunk advertisement) cries Betty.   "No,"
says Jack, "we can buy what we need in New York"
(Biltmore Hotel); "all we need is money" (American
Express Cheques), "and a few necessities" (William's
Shaving Stick, Pepsodent, and the rest).   He glances
at his automobile (Mercer), sees that the tires (United
States) are in condition for a fast run, and helping
Betty in, lights a cigarette (Camels), and in another
moment the car has passed out of sight ("for fine
roads use Tarvia").

It is, I think, rather curious that it is only recently
that the National Association of Booksellers has con-

sidered advertising in a manner designed to increase
the demand, not for any one special book, but for
books in general; not for the product of any one publisher on sale at any particular shop, but advertising
the object of which is to stimulate the habit of buying
books — new books, old books, in a word, "anything
that's a book." Of course it can be done. It will
take time and money, but it is well worth doing.

Now for the sake of the discussion let me suggest a
slogan — *Buy a Book a Week*.   There are millions to
whom this slogan will make no appeal, but there are
millions who will be attracted by it — or a better one;
millions who are not accustomed to buy books, and
who will at first regard the slogan with amazement
and as not intended for them. The power of itera-
tion and reiteration is not yet fully understood: it is
worthy of, and doubtless has received, the attention
of the psychologist.   Gradually it will be made to
appear that it is as disgraceful not to buy a book a
week as it is to wear a celluloid collar or to use a gold
toothpick.   At present it occurs to relatively few
people to buy books: tell them to, keep on telling
them to; and after a while they will.   And when a
man is by way of forming the habit of buying books
and reading them, you may tell him why he is doing
so, and what he should buy, and whence.[1]

Why should we read?   Book-lovers have spent
much time inventing finely flowing sentences in reply

[1] Inspired, perhaps, by the first appearance of this chapter, a well-
known Boston bookseller offered a prize for the best poem on its
theme. Among the verses submitted in the competition were these: —

to this question, which is more frequently answered than asked. Augustine Birrell, that fine old bookman, in a paragraph which betrays no effort at smartness, says in the preface to his edition of Boswell's "Life of Johnson": "Literature is meant to give pleasure, to excite interest, to banish solitude, to make the fireside more attractive than the tavern, to give joy to those who are still capable of joy, and — why should we not admit it? — to drug sorrow, and divert thought." There is in this something of sadness — old age speaks, rather than youth; but it is a very fine summary of the purpose of literature.

Before me on my writing-table is a dainty, dumpy volume, bound in white cloth, and very much soiled, having for title, "The Book-Lover's Enchiridion."

A BOOK A WEEK

A book a week! I heave a sigh;
That Slogan's peremptory cry
I will not hear, I will not heed.
How can *They* say that I should need
The book *They* bid me weekly buy ?

But Slogans change, as days go by;
My Psyche listens, fluttering shy,
To newer message — "Come and *Read*
    A book a week."

To read! to read! O wings that fly
O'er sun-kissed lands, through clouded sky,
That bear us on where Great ones lead!
I too must follow, so I plead
For magic wings. I'll read (or try)
    A book a week!

It was given by its compiler, Alexander Ireland, to Mrs. James T. Fields, "with sincere and heartfelt regards"; and as it contains all of the best things ever said in praise of books and reading, I have, since I had this subject in mind, read it through from cover to cover, hoping that I might get from it a note of inspiration for this paper; but I have not done so. No, the "Enchiridion" is designed for the use and delectation of those who already understand the love of books. Many a time I have taken it up for ten or twenty minutes when I should have been in bed; but the excerpts of which it is composed are too exquisite, too dainty, too imaginative, for my present purpose, which is to suggest that a man in the street may be shamed at the thought that he has no books. Of what use is it to tell such a one, as Emerson does, "Consider what you have in the smallest chosen library. A company of the wisest and wittiest men that could be picked out of all countries in a thousand years." I, sitting in my library, am flattered that such a statement appeals to me: it suggests that I feel at home in such company; but tell the average man in a hurry that, if he will pause for a moment, he may meet "the wisest and wittiest," and he will reply, "I should worry," or some such inanity, and pass on.

No! a man must be told flatly, peremptorily, to *Buy a Book a Week*, and — not at first, but after a time — he will do it. Clubs might be formed and buttons worn; and long before this point is reached, indeed at the very outset, the whole subject should

be turned over to the best expert advertising opinion, that the matter may be carefully studied.   This
will take time and money, but the thing need not be
done in a hurry; the book-trade has survived for
centuries without such stimulation as I am suggesting.   A year may well be spent in preparing such a
campaign; as for the money, there should be no difficulty : a small fraction of one per cent of the total
book-sales of the country should be levied on every
bookseller, wholesale as well as retail — from such
an important publisher as Macmillan in New York
to such a high eccentric retailer as George Rigby in
Philadelphia.   This tax should produce such a sum
as would secure the best advertising talent in the
country.

"Do it electrically" has long been a slogan in the
game with which I am in some measure familiar.
Do what?   Anything : melt copper or freeze cream;
drive a ship or a needle.   *"Buy a Book a Week."* [1]
What book?   Any book,— "The Four Horsemen"
or "The Education of Henry Adams," — and sooner
or later we shall have a book-buying public, not
merely a group of scattered individuals, to whom "a
home without books is like a room without windows."

The study of advertising is the study of national

---

[1] Some time after this "slogan" had been given national publicity, I
received a letter from a friend, reading as follows : "That wretched
slogan of yours is rapidly working my ruin. Last week I bought a first
Shakespeare's Poems for forty-five hundred dollars; this week I bought
a first *Paradise Lost* for three thousand dollars; next week I shall
buy a presentation *Hamlet*. God knows how much I shall have to
pay for it."

temperaments. Advertising is a form of boasting, and we Americans are the greatest advertisers in the world: the French know little or nothing of it, and the English relatively little. "Privacy" is their watchword; "publicity" is ours. If one wants a thing in England, one has to hunt for it; with us, the greatest difficulty is to escape from things one does not want. Advertising is, in general, but little understood. We all advertise; a silk hat and a box at the opera are forms of advertising,— by such means one advertises one's arrival in society,— but a professional man must be more subtle than a tradesman. I have always maintained that a successful tradesman is more to be envied than any other person in the world: he is not obliged to wear a silk hat; he advertises frankly, "Here are candles, three for a penny"; the inference is, take them or leave them.

But we were speaking of slogans. Think for a moment of the force of a catchword or phrase many million times repeated. Politicians spend much time inventing slogans, but no one used them more successfully than Roosevelt, with his "Predatory Rich" and his "Big Stick" and a hundred others. In general, slogans stick; they may be used as a foundation on which a superstructure of publicity may be erected, or as the capstone of an advertising campaign.

From my point of view, any word or phrase or picture or thing that is identified with or instantly calls to mind another thing is a slogan. Does any American, steaming past the Rock of Gibraltar, see it without thinking of a certain insurance company, or see the whiff of steam floating from a white marble pyramid as he enters New York Harbor without associating it with a trust company of almost limitless resources? "You push the button"; "Ask the man who owns one"; "It floats" — there are hundreds and thousands of them, bits of property of almost incalculable value, because they are recorded in the minds of millions, rather than because they are registered in the United States Patent Office.

I cannot believe that any enlightened association, such as the American Booksellers' Association is, will ever use, whatever advertising method it adopts, the out-of-doors signs which are such blisters upon our landscape. As if to make the approach to our cities and towns more hideous than they already are, "concessions" are secured and immense signs erected, calling attention to the merits of someone's oil as a lubricant, either for one's motor or one's bowels. Such advertising is positively loathsome, and sooner or later it will be stopped. Question my friend Joe Pennell's methods if you will (I have heard him spoken of as one who never said a kind word or did an unkind thing to anyone), he is certainly right when he says that these great signs are a national disgrace and should be taxed out of existence. And in times like these, when lumber for legitimate building is expensive and transportation difficult, it is almost a crime to use millions of feet of lumber in erecting these hideous defilements of our highways. Should a man stand outside my gate and beat a drum night and day, he would ultimately be taken either to a hospital or to an undertaker's; and those who make our country hideous with their shrieking signs should suffer the same fate. As for bill-board advertising, the case of our towns is indeed desperate; but I am not altogether without hope.

There are plenty of proper advertising media: of newspapers and magazines, having a total circulation of hundreds of millions, there is no lack; while, in spite of the fact that the unskilled laborer now has his automobile, many of us still hang on straps in trolley-cars, and our minds might well be stimulated the while. And I do not despair of bookshop windows being made at least as attractive as those displaying — what shall I say? — men's hats. Let me expand this idea a little, if idea it is. Shop-windows have an immense advertising value; too frequently they are decorated by the shipping clerk, on a principle which I have never clearly understood. I offer the following suggestion.

Let a window (always the same window), or a portion of a window (always the same portion),— against a background of best sellers, if necessary; but I suggest a silken, sad, uncertain curtain,— be devoted always to a display relating to some author, the anniversary of whose birthday or death-day is approaching.

For example, take Rudyard Kipling — with the exception of Thomas Hardy, the most distinguished literary man now living. Suppose that on December 30, 1921, we secure a photograph or other portrait and announce on a suitable card, "Rudyard Kipling

JOSEPH PENNELL, OUR GREAT ARTIST

Sketched during one of his less cantankerous moods by F. Walter Taylor. While I was debating whether I could afford to buy this portrait, my son secured it and sent me the bill, thus relieving me of the difficulty of coming to a decision

is 56 years old to-day." Then suppose that we surround the man with his works — first editions, autograph letters, souvenirs, etc., if available; and if they are not in stock, perhaps, if we are in Philadelphia, and on good terms with the owner of such a superb collection as Ellis Ames Ballard's, we may secure the loan for a day or two of a few items that will cause the initiated in such matters to rub his eyes in amazement.

The idea may be expanded, and details added, to such an extent that, in course of time, that constantly changing exhibit will be a liberal education. It will have a drawing power that people will be unable to resist. They will cross the street to look at it; they will think of it and speak of it, and be glad to establish relations with its owners. How pleased we are when the head waiter of a well-established restaurant addresses us by name when we enter! A bookshop may hold the same thrill for us.

But you may say, "All this costs money and takes time; I have no one available for such a job." My reply is that such work could be syndicated and its cost divided among many. Miss Bessie Graham, already an honorary member of the American Booksellers' Association and well known by reason of her classes and papers on Bookselling, is admirably fitted to superintend the preparation and distribution of such suggestions as would be timely, stimulating, and helpful.

Bookshops can and should furnish a sort of postgraduate course in literature. Let the campaign of

education go forward : and let us so carry it on that
every he or she who reads may run — to the nearest
bookshop. I am not an advertising agency. Dr. Johnson called advertising a trade; I should call it a profession, rather. The subject should be carefully studied
by someone of special aptitude and training.

DE:PARTMENTAL
DITTIES
AND OTHER
VERSES

No. 1 of 1886.

To

all Heads of Depa

and all Anglo-Indians

Rudyard Kipling ASSISTANT,

Department of Public Journalism,

Lahore District.

AN EARLY KIPLING ITEM "WITH THE FLAP"

VI

"'T IS NOT IN MORTALS TO COMMAND SUCCESS."

INDEED it is not, nor has "deserving" anything whatever to do with it. We who, by dint of saving here and scraping there, manage at the end of twenty years or so to have a respectable collection of books, know that the battle is not always to the brave, but generally to the side of the heaviest artillery; for this is no puny game we collectors are playing, and we are playing it against giants. I am not alluding to those men who, with the instincts and fortunes of the Medici, get their names in the paper every day; I refer to the collector who quietly, almost stealthily, goes on, day after day and year after year, buying in some well-defined line, until at last he — and sometimes shé — may be said to have everything. But this is only in the way of speaking, for no collection is ever complete; one may drop dead in the race with the goal not yet in sight; that's where the excitement lies.

Such thoughts as these came into my head when, some time ago, I spent several days with a man in Buffalo, a man so modest and retiring that not all of his friends know that he has the greatest collection of Johnson and Boswell material in the world. I refer, of course, to Mr. R. B. Adam.[1] Sixteen years ago

[1] See illustration opposite page 74.

Mr. Adam inherited from his father, the late Robert B. Adam, the finest collection of Johnsoniana in the world.

As I am accused of being given to exaggeration whenever I speak of Dr. Johnson, let me hasten to say that this is not my opinion only, but that it was the mature judgment of that great Johnsonian editor, Birkbeck Hill. In a paper printed many years ago in the "Atlantic Monthly," and subsequently delivered in a somewhat changed form before the Johnson Club in London, Dr. Hill said : —

"On the shores of Lake Erie, in the flourishing town of Buffalo, I found a finer collection of Johnsonian and Boswellian curiosities than exists elsewhere on our side of the Atlantic." He then went on to describe at length what he saw, adding, "Great as has been the liberality of some of our collectors in letting me see their stores, Mr. Adam in his liberality has far surpassed them all. . . . The devout Johnsonian may count on receiving a warm welcome . . . and the shrine will be thrown open to him. . . . I shall never join in the lament that is raised among us Englishmen when autographs and rare editions of our great writers are bought by an American."

With these words in my head and a visiting card in my hand, I presented myself to the present Adam some few years ago. Twenty-seven years have passed since Dr. Hill's experience, but there has been no change in the family manner. Instantly I was made to feel at home, and a warm friendship has been the result of an almost chance meeting. Indeed, I am always suspicious of the man to whom Samuel Johnson does not make appeal, and I have never met a good Johnsonian who was not a good fellow.

But if there has been no falling off in the kindly hospitality of the Adam family, important additions have been made to the collection by its present owner. A Johnson or a Boswell item of supreme interest comes to the surface in London, New York, or elsewhere. It is for a moment conspicuous and then disappears, subsequently to reappear — in Buffalo. I am something of a Johnsonian myself. Ever since I first read Boswell's "Life of Johnson" in Napier's admirable edition, in 1884, I have kept a copy near at hand to dip into, always with pleasure and with profit; but when I was given the "freedom of the city," so to speak, of Mr. Adam's collection, I knew there was no place for me in that line, and I turned to Oliver Goldsmith, with the same result; for I came to know that Mr. William M. Elkins of Philadelphia was on the lookout for first editions of everything that Goldsmith had written, until at last, he got them all — all except one item, the "Threnodia Augustalis," of which only two copies are known; and finally one of these two fell before his practically unlimited bid at the Wallace Sale — that holocaust which took place in New York in the winter of 1920.

I never look at that fine old mezzotint of Goldsmith across the room without thinking of my purchase of it from George Rigby. I dropped in on him one day and saw the print, saw that it was in good condition, and asked him the price.

"Thirty dollars," said George; "but I have laid it aside for your friend Hawley McLanahan."

"Has he seen it? Have you told him about it?" I inquired.

"No," said George, "but he will buy it; he's rather going in for these eighteenth-century prints."

The print was worth a hundred. Taking from my pocket three ten-dollar bills, for money talks even in so uncommercial an establishment as Rigby's, I told him to roll up the print. As he was doing so, rather reluctantly, George said, "You won't say anything about it to McLanahan?"

"Oh, won't I!" I replied; "you shall hear from him, and promptly."

When I got back to my office, I called Mac on the phone and told him that if he had any more of that brand of Scotch for which he was famous, I would stop in during the evening and tell him a good story.

"Come along," he said; "the bottle shall be on the table by the time you get here."

With the wisdom of a man from Aberdeen, I let several glasses of the divine liquor trickle down my throat, and then, and not until then, I told him the story of my purchase.

It did not take me long to discover that I was too late to become either a Goldsmith collector or to write an essay about him, and yet I should like to do both : out of pity and of love. Goldsmith has always been misunderstood — in his own day, because he was

OLIVER GOLDSMITH
After the portrait by Sir Joshua Reynolds

an Irishman, and in ours, on account of that impromptu epitaph of Garrick,—

> Here lies Nolly Goldsmith, for shortness called "Noll,"
> Who wrote like an angel but talk'd like poor Poll.

Nothing can be more damaging to a reputation than a stinging couplet. Crime can be lived down — indeed, certain crimes give one a sort of distinction; but once start a couplet rolling, and it gathers momentum until it crushes all who oppose it. A good example of this is supplied by the epigram of the Earl of Rochester, written on the bedroom door of Charles II : —

> Here lies our Sovereign Lord the King,
> Whose word no man relies on;
> He never says a foolish thing
> Or ever does a wise one.

In vain did Charles attempt the explanation that his words were his own while his acts were his ministers': it all went for naught. But I am not in the least interested in the reputation of the Royal Charles, whereas Goldsmith's is inexpressibly dear to me.

Boswell did not like Goldsmith — indeed, did not understand him; and Johnson, although he greatly admired him, did not fully understand him, either. The best retort in Boswell's book is Goldsmith's reply to Johnson when he said that, if he were writing a fable, he would make his animals talk in character: he would make little fishes talk like little fishes. Johnson, whose sides were shaking with laughter at the turn the conversation had taken, could not have been altogether pleased when Goldy said: "Why, Dr.

Johnson, this is not so easy as you seem to think, for if you were to make little fishes talk, they would talk like whales." And it was Goldsmith, too, who, when someone called Johnson a bear, replied, very justly: "He has, to be sure, a certain roughness in his manner, but no man alive has a more tender heart. He has nothing of the bear but his skin." And when someone called Boswell a *cur*, which he certainly was not, Goldsmith at once corrected it to *burr*, saying he has the quality of sticking. Yet Boswell is constantly talking of Goldsmith's misfortunes in conversation; and whenever his name is mentioned, one almost unconsciously repeats to one's self Garrick's silly couplet.

Foiled in the direction of Johnson and Goldsmith, I looked over the field of my favorites. Byron: Mr. Morgan has them all, every one. Shelley: too voluminous and running into thousands before a fair start is had; when Mr. Thomas J. Wise shows you his "Shelleys," you simply expire with envy. Lamb: Mr. Spoor's carriage blocks the way; it is a carriage only by courtesy, it being in fact a well-furnished van. Oscar Wilde: it is quite useless; John B. Stetson has everything. Tennyson: I have not forgotten that rare day I spent in Mr. W. H. Arnold's library, looking over his Tennyson material; progress in that direction is impossible. Keats: here I collide with Miss Amy Lowell, with the usual result.

But something may yet be done. Let me reconnoitre a bit. There is Leigh Hunt. It is, of course, a sad falling off; but is there a book-lover who has not in his heart a soft spot for him? I admit that his

MASK OF DAVID GARRICK, BY R. E. PINE

From rare mezzotint

books are patchy and gossipy, but he was a man of taste, if not of learning, and a delightful companion, and who does not know that a delightful companion is harder to find than a scholar? Scholarship may be taught. He wrote of "Men, Women, and Books" — the three things best worth writing about. How I wish I could have paid him for his books, instead of the booksellers! How pleased he would be to think of himself as "collected." Poor fellow! fancy having to support a wife in poor health and a constantly increasing crop of children by writing such books as "Imagination and Fancy," and "The Old Court Suburb," and "A Jar of Honey"! Is it any wonder that he was not robust in money matters, and that he regarded a financial transaction as completed when he had given his I. O. U. for it. I have been brought up in a more practical school, but I never close the lid of my desk and, under the plea of important business, go off to a book-auction, without recalling his remark: "How satisfactory it is to think of others nobly doing their duty while I am following the bent of my own inclinations."

If not for himself, Leigh Hunt will always be remembered as an intimate friend of the three poets who made the first quarter of the nineteenth century forever memorable: Byron, with whom he finally quarreled — temperamentally they had nothing in common; Shelley, whom he loved and by whose funeral pyre he watched; and Keats, whose genius he was the first to recognize. It was Hunt who, in May, 1816, in his "Examiner," gave Keats his first appearance in print. During that year Keats and Hunt were close companions, and at the home of the latter in Hampstead, they read and wrote much together and lived in a world of "Imagination and Fancy." On December 1, Hunt published in his paper Keats's now famous sonnet, "On First Looking into Chapman's Homer"; and on that same day Hunt addressed to Keats a sonnet in which he prophesied that he would wear the laurel. Keats kept the poem by him, and it was found by Severn among his papers after his death. The original manuscript is in my possession, and from it I quote.

TO JOHN KEATS

'T is well you think me truly one of those
Whose sense discerns the loveliness of things;
For surely as I feel the bird that sings
Behind the leaves, or the Kiss-asking rose,
Or the rich bee, rejoicing as he goes,
Or the glad issue of emerging springs,
Or, overhead, the glide of a dove's wings,
Or trees, or turf, or midst of all repose:
And surely as I feel things lovelier still,
The human look — and the harmonious form
Containing Woman — and the smile in ill,
And such a heart as Charles's, wise and warm,
As surely as all this, I see e'en now,
Young Keats, a flowering laurel on your brow.

HAMPSTEAD, *Dec.* 1, 1816.

"One of the most interesting personalities I have met in America," is the way a distinguished Englishman described Miss Lowell to me after a visit to her in Boston. I can readily understand how he reached this conclusion, for she reminds one only of herself.

SONNET TO JOHN KEATS, BY LEIGH HUNT
From the original manuscript

She is a busy woman, not altogether easy to approach; but if she meets you at all, it is with the hearty welcome of a man with the charm of a woman, for this *femme savante* is a woman of the world and of many moods. It has been my privilege to see something of her in her lighter hours, to listen and to talk to her,— not of her poetry, I am of the school of Pope,— but of her library. "Do you want to see my Blakes or my Keats?"— and she can hold your attention with either,— she will say, leading you into a fine old room overflowing with books. "Let us work up to speed gradually; why start on high?" you will answer— only to be told that she is "geared that way." Remembering my dear old Quaker friend Cadbury, who proudly carries around in his pocket an essay by Miss Lowell in the form of a letter on the "Rollo" books, you suggest that you begin with Rollo — on the Atlantic, or elsewhere; and in a moment you are off — "on high" — in spite of yourself; and when a few moments later you look at your watch, it is long after midnight. "No matter," she will say, "there will be a motor for you, and the evening has just begun." And when, the hours being no longer wee, you finally take your leave of her, you bid her, not "Goodnight," but "Good-morning."

Miss Lowell began forming her library many years ago, under the direction of the elder Quaritch; and I can quite understand that, when she breezed into his shop in Piccadilly, he gave her the run of the place and allowed her to make her own prices. Accustomed as he was to lords and dukes and to the ways of

American millionaires, this young girl, so alert and
clever and winsome, must have made the old man
rub his eyes and wonder whether there were many
Boston girls like her. Someone must have told him
that there were not. I can
see him giving her a cup
of tea, which she would
condescend to sip only because it gave her a chance
to wheedle out of the
keeping of the shrewd old
bookman the three slen-
der Keats volumes which
— with one love-affair —
made up his entire life.

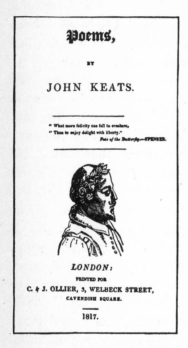

"Here are several son-
nets and the original
manuscript of 'The Eve of
St. Agnes,'" Miss Lowell
will say, placing them in
your hands; and you will
feel a gentle thrill as you
turn the soft pages, re-
membering that you are gazing upon immortal poetry.
And then she will show the silver medal, with his
name engraved thereon, which he won for "voluntary
work" when a lad at Mr. Clarke's Academy at
Enfield. Finally, you may be permitted to read,
perhaps, in her "Lamia," which the poet gave to
Fanny Brawne — in the whole realm of association
books, one of the finest.

JOHN KEATS

From original portrait by Severn, sometimes referred to as the " lost portrait."

I have always admitted that it was Miss Lowell's enthusiasm for Keats that led me into a financial morass, when the serpent in the shape of Dr. Rosenbach placed before me for inspection a collection of Keats material that the elder Sabin had been years in assembling. In recent years all my financial distress has been connected with Rosy. To be sure, he said very little — there was no occasion; he pointed out that this was my opportunity; in brief, "The serpent beguiled me and I did eat." What have I? Well, without boasting, I have faultless first editions of the three slender

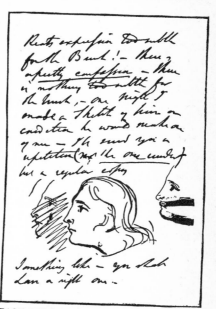

PAGE (MUCH REDUCED) FROM A LETTER OF BENJAMIN ROBERT HAYDON TO ELIZABETH BARRETT (BROWNING) 1834.

volumes (but alas, no presentation copies; Mr. Elkins out-bid me on the last lot sold at auction), and two love letters to Fanny Brawne; the manuscript of one poem and a fine cluster of autograph letters from Browning, and Mrs. Browning, Rossetti, Monckton Milnes, Tennyson, and others, relating to the poet; and the earliest portrait known of Keats, at the age of fifteen — a dainty little silhouette height-

ened with gold, reproduced by Sir Sidney Colvin
in his edition of the poet's works. Nor is this all.
I have a lovely portrait in colored crayons of the
poet, his head leaning on his hand, with an inscription: "John Keats by J. Severn, from life, found
among my father's papers. Walter Severn, 1880."

The centenary of the death of John Keats, who
died on February 23, 1821, lends especial interest to
the death-bed portrait by his friend Joseph Severn.
Truth to tell, Severn was not a great painter, but his
name will ever be remembered as the friend of one of
England's greatest poets, by whose death-bed he
watched, and near whom he is buried.

The sketch reproduced is perhaps better known
than any other portrait of Keats. It was at once
recognized that Severn had caught the spiritual
beauty of the poet as he lay dying, and the drawing
becoming famous, several copies of the original were
made; one of these is in the Keats-Shelley Memorial
at Rome, and another may be seen in one of the great
private libraries of New York.

My reproduction is made from the original drawing,
which was secured by a well-known London bookseller some years ago at the dispersal of the effects of
Walter Severn, the son of the artist, who had re-
tained it, and from which the several replicas were
made. The faint wording beneath the sketch reads:
"28 Jany. 3 o'clock Mng. drawn to keep me awake —
a deadly sweat was on him all this night."

The grave of Keats in the Protestant Burial
Ground in Rome is visited each year by an increasing

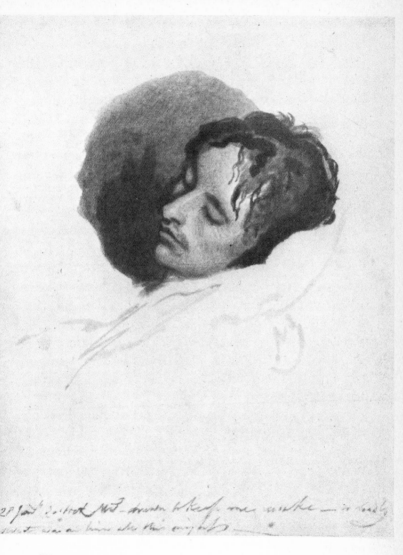

DEATH–BED PORTRAIT OF JOHN KEATS, BY JOSEPH SEVERN

number of pilgrims, anxious to do homage to the memory of the poet who desired that his epitaph should be, "Here lies one whose name was writ in water." Shelley's reference to this line is well known.

By the time I had secured these and several more, I supposed that my collection of Keats portraits left little to be desired, until I received a letter from Sawyer, the London bookseller, offering me the original plaster portrait of Keats by Girometti, which had once belonged to Keats's intimate friend Haslam, with a letter from Sir Sidney Colvin testifying to its authenticity. This I was glad to have, as it is the

THE EVE OF ST. MARK
From the original manuscript, taken down in shorthand from Keats's dictation to his friend Woodhouse

original from which was made the marble medallion that is familiar to those who have made pilgrimages to the Protestant Cemetery in Rome. Something tells me that, when I next meet my friend Nelson Gay in Rome, he will offer to relieve me of the care of some of these treasures; and if I can ever bring myself to part with any of these, I know of no place more fitting for them than the Keats-Shelley Museum at Rome, for this is one of the few small museums in which treasures of this character would not be swallowed up and absolutely lost.   There were several interesting Keats letters to Fanny Brawne sold one evening not long ago at the Anderson Galleries in New York, which led to the writing of this sonnet by Christopher Morley, which he gave me leave to reprint rather than what he calls his "youthful indiscretion," which appears elsewhere.

IN AN AUCTION ROOM

"How about this lot?" said the auctioneer,
  "One hundred, may I say, just for a start?"

  Between the plum-red curtains, drawn apart,
  A written sheet was held. . . . And strange to hear

  (Dealer, would I were steadfast as thou art),
  The cold quick bids ("Against you in the rear!")
  The crimson salon, in a glow more clear
  Burned bloodlike purple as the poet's heart.

  Song that outgrew the singer! Bitter Love
  That broke the proud hot heart it held in thrall —

  Poor script, where still those tragic passions move —
  Eight hundred bid; fair warning; the last call;
  The soul of Adonais, like a star. . . .
  Soul for eight hundred dollars —"Doctor R!"

It so happens that I have the manuscript of Oscar Wilde's sonnet on "The Grave of Keats," as well as the sonnet by Rossetti on "Keats Sixty Years

THE GRAVES OF JOHN KEATS AND JOSEPH SEVERN IN THE PROTESTANT
CEMETERY IN ROME

Dead." Both of these, in my judgment, are distinctly inferior to the poem given above, which, in addition to doing justice to Keats's song, "that outgrew the singer," is cleverly reminiscent of the auction-room.

Oliver Goldsmith

VII

LET the scholar or the antiquary decide when
English literature begins; for me it begins, not at the
beginning, but with Chaucer. Of what went before,
my impressions are vague and uncertain; but Chaucer
sometimes seems almost as alive to me as anyone in
"Who's Who," particularly when, after a weary winter, spring comes at last, and the birds begin to sing,
and the leaves unfold themselves upon the trees.
I say to myself, "It was on such a day as this that
Chaucer's pilgrims set out." "On such a day as
this," whether the sky is blue, flecked with clouds of
white, or "Aprille" threatens us with her customary
showers; for when the world was young, as it was five
hundred years ago, an "Aprille" shower would surely
not have deterred any one of the nine-and-twenty
pilgrims from mounting his or her palfrey in the yard
of the Tabard Inn and journeying on to the shrine of
the murdered Archbishop, St. Thomas à Becket, at
Canterbury. But the English in which Chaucer wrote
makes it more or less difficult for any except the student to understand him; and while Coleridge says
that, after reading twenty pages with a glossary, there
will be no further difficulty, reading with a glossary is
not reading but studying, and alas, how few of us care
to study after our school and college days are over!

And after Chaucer, I leap a whole century and a half to Shakespeare, skipping Spenser, the scholars', poets' poet, remembering the lines,—

> No profit grows where is no pleasure ta'en,
> In brief, Sir, study what you most affect,—

which I have always done. Of Shakespeare, it is hardly for me to speak except from the viewpoint of the collector; and Shakespeare has now become almost impossible except for the very rich. Let but a few years pass, and all the desirable quartos, and even the folios, will have passed into that bourne whence no book returns — the great public library. How rapidly they are going is, perhaps, understood only by those who are curious in such matters. Of late we have heard much of Mr. Huntington's buying this, of Mr. Folger's buying that, and of Mr. Cochran's buying t'other, and of the immense sums they are giving for rare books; but these gentlemen are not spending their money selfishly. Mr. Cochran, we know, buys for that wonderful institution which he has established and maintains — the Elizabethan Club at Yale;[1] Mr. Huntington's books have gone to the State of California; and it is safe to say that Mr. Folger's collection will never be dispersed. These are, in effect, public libraries, and in paying seemingly high prices, their owners are making gifts of just so much money to the public. I often ask myself whether the public fully appreciates the value of these gifts.

This is an age of libraries, and I never enter such

[1] Mr. Newton was elected an honorary member of the Elizabethan Club in April, 1921.

buildings as the Congressional Library in Washington and the public libraries of New York, Boston, Chicago (I wish I could add Philadelphia), without wondering whether, in the centuries to come, they will ever have the charm for the student that so many of the old-world libraries have for us to-day; or whether, after our habit, they will be torn down and larger and even more magnificent buildings erected.

But I had it in mind to write a page or two on the subject of Shakespeare quartos. Only the initiated understand the feeling that arises in the heart of the collector at the word "quartos" — those slender little tracts of thirty pages or so, containing single plays, which are to-day so greatly esteemed that the rarest of them can no longer be had for the hundreds of a few years ago, but now run into thousands of dollars — or even pounds, if you like that denomination better. I sometimes think the popularity of the quarto is due in no small measure to its size. It is such a handy little book, easily referred to; it can be collated, or studied, or shown to a friend, without the necessity of clearing off a table. I know a man, John L. Clawson of Buffalo, who, if he did not have so many other rare books, might be said to collect nothing but quarto plays; and he shows them, and rightly too, as if they were Whistler etchings.

Before me on my writing-table there is a set of proofs of a catalogue soon to be published by the Rosenbach Company, to inaugurate the opening of its new establishment in New York City. There are only twenty-nine items in it, but it is, nevertheless, one of the most remarkable book-catalogues ever printed; for it is entirely devoted to Shakespeare quartos, and the prices for common, or garden, varieties range from $500, for a late "Julius Cæsar," to $32,500 for an unbound and uncut "Pericles"; while a "Troilus and Cressida" may yet be had for $12,500. This, we are told, is known as the "Prologue Issue," because of the prophecy expressed therein of the great demand that will ensue for these quartos after Shakespeare's death. It is indeed startling in its aptness; it reads: "*When he is gone and his comedies out of sale, you will scramble for them.*" With values running to something like a thousand dollars a page, I would say that the scramble is almost over, and that any further proceedings will partake of the nature of a triumphal procession.

I once heard of a person beginning a conversation by a repartee. In like manner, I find that I have introduced my own almost lonely quarto by an anti-climax. The story of my little book begins in that delicious Old-World library, the Bodleian at Oxford — as far removed from the firing-line of affairs as it is possible to get. There, in the splendid collection of quartos, once the property of that distinguished Shakespearean scholar and collector, Edmund Malone, is a rare "Hamlet," on the fly-leaf of which is written by its former owner, "This edition was printed, I believe, in 1607." I have just spent a pleasant hour reading in a copy of this same edition, now generally known as the "undated Hamlet." It is one of my recent acquisitions, and according to

Bartlett & Pollard's "Census" — and there is no higher authority — is one of only six copies in private hands, the few other known copies being safely anchored in public libraries.

The genesis of such a play as "Hamlet" is one of the most interesting things in bibliographical history. The first edition of "Hamlet" (1603) is very far from being the play as we know it: it has only 2143 lines, as against 3719 lines in the second edition (1604), on which, together with the first folio edition (1623), the acting version of to-day is based. Mr. Huntington divides with the British Museum, on the basis of fifty-fifty, the honors of the first edition. His copy, to be sure, lacks the last leaf, but, on the other hand, the British Museum copy lacks the title-page; so the advantage, if any, is with us. But it is probable that, in spite of Malone, the "undated Hamlet" is not the third edition, but rather the edition of 1611. However this may be, my "Hamlet" is a very pretty bibliographical treasure, coming as it does from the Marsden J. Perry collection of Shakespeareana, which Dr. Rosenbach purchased *en bloc* and dispersed almost before we knew what he was doing.[1]

[1] My *Hamlet* is unbound; that is not to say it is in sheets, for it has been bound, probably in a volume of old plays, and closely cropped. Having once been bound, its present appearance is not elegant, and it is desirable that it should be put in substantial covers. So to Marguerite Lahey of New York (out of Paris, as a stud-book would say) it shall go, without instructions other than that she is to make the binding worthy of the intellectual and intrinsic value of the book. I seek not to know in advance what the cost will be, or when it will be finished; for Miss Lahey is one of the world's greatest binders, and is not to be hurried. She is not an accomplished amateur, as some might

THE
TRAGEDY
OF
HAMLET
Prince of Denmarke.

Newly Imprinted and inlarged, according to the true
and perfect Copy lastly Printed.

BY
WILLIAM SHAKESPEARE.

LONDON,
Printed by W. S. for *John Smethwicke*, and are to be sold at his
Shop in Saint *Dunstans* Church-yard in Fleetstreet:
Vnder the Diall.

THE RARE QUARTO "HAMLET," KNOWN TO COLLECTORS
AS THE "UNDATED HAMLET"

When Rosy moves, it is difficult to follow him —
difficult, nay, it is frequently impossible.

I have always tried to steer clear of such books as
these, regarding them as dangerous rocks lying on
either side of the narrow channel which I try to navi-
gate, against which my fragile bark may be dashed
to pieces in an instant. But "Hamlet" is such a wonderful play! And I never think of it but I see in
imagination those two volumes compact with learning, the variorum "Hamlet" of the late Dr. Furness,
beloved by all who knew him; and I never meet his
son but there comes into my mind a line out of
Pope's translation of the Iliad,— or the Odyssey, I
forget which; I have not read either for more than
forty years,—

> Few sons inherit the wisdom of their great sires,
> And most their sires' disgrace.

Certainly he is of the few. In this Philadelphia
family, as in the Adams family of which Boston is so
proud, scholarship appears to be a birthright.

Horace J. Bridges, in his most enjoyable book,
"Our Fellow Shakespeare" ("Why here's our fellow
Shakespeare puts them all downe!" — *The Returne
from Pernassus*, 1606), says: "The child ought to
start by loving 'Hamlet' for the sake of the Ghost,
the poisoning, the usurpation, the entrapping of
Rosencrantz and Guildenstern, the fencing-match,

for a moment suppose, but a woman of learning and great skill in her
art, and of impeccable taste. This is not my opinion merely,— my
opinion in the matter of bindings is almost worthless,— but it is the
mature judgment of such connoisseurs as Belle da Costa Greene, Miss
Thurston, and others expert in such matters.

the poisoned rapiers, and the envenomed wine-cup."
This is exactly the spot at which I began. It was in
1876, the year of the Centennial Exposition, and I
was twelve years old. I remember the time and the
place: it was on a Sunday evening, the family had all
gone to church, and I was quite alone in the house;
and when I came to the lines,—

> I am thy father's spirit
> Doom'd for a certain term to walk the night,
> And for the day confin'd to fast in fires,—

I thought that, if the family did not soon come home
from church, a little boy would be missing when they
did — and yet I could not put the book down. For
three centuries, on the stage and in the closet,
"Hamlet" has been the supreme play; one never
tires of it, one knows it almost by heart, and instead
of reading it, one finds one's self reciting those passages which have almost lost their significance, so
hackneyed they have become. What a thrill must
have passed through lords and groundlings at the old
Globe Theatre when these immortal words were ut-
tered for the first time: "To be or not to be"; or

> The time is out of joint: O cursed spite,
> That ever I was born to set it right.

And that's where I have the advantage of Hamlet,
or of any prince whatever; for I was not so born, and
I sometimes wonder whether the time is not always
out of joint; our time certainly is — owing in no
small measure, as it seems to me, to the obstinacy of
a little group of one willful man; and if it be objected
that one man cannot properly be called a group, let

me reply that, when that man is the President of the United States, he counts double or triple, or as many as you will. What page in the last court grammar made him a plural is not for me to inquire.

And now I remember that I am writing on the 4th of March, 1920. One year from to-day the President will slink out of the White House and pass into history, where his idiosyncrasies can be studied at leisure; and at the same hour, another man will drop the pleasant *cameraderie* of the candidate and, assuming the insolence of office (though in this respect he is unlikely to match the present incumbent), will proceed to govern us in such manner as will redound to his greatest personal advantage and ensure him a second term in office. And to this end, we, every so often, permit ourselves to become enthusiastic, and form clubs, and even march in the streets, wearing silk hats, under the delusion that we are influencing the course of events.

In times like these, what a relief it is to close the door upon the world, with its wrangling and recrimination, and enter that other cosmos — the world of books; that substantial world around which, as Wordsworth says, "our pastime and our happiness will grow." Is there not some scrap of paper, not yet totally destroyed, granting us life, liberty, and an opportunity for the pursuit of that will-o'-the-wisp, happiness? I sometimes think that I have found it in my library. When I can be sure, I shall announce the fact; but this much is certain: I am happier here than elsewhere in the world, unless it be in London; and what is London but a book, in which is written everything that can by any possible chance interest an intelligent person speaking English as his mother-tongue?

What a delight it is, at the end of a busy day, to throw one's self into an arm-chair before a wood fire, and think. No, not think! muse is a better word. I am by no means sure that I've ever thought, and I'm not certain that I wish to; looking about me, I see thinkers, and it does not appear that they are either wiser or better or happier than I. What has all the mental truck and sweat of the thinkers of Germany amounted to? "The land of the damned professor!" Indeed, one does not have to say that Germany to a man was wrong; there were probably a few commonplace business men, like myself, who did not like the drift of things; but certainly their heavy thinkers have made a sad mess of it. By taking thought they seemed to add cubits to their stature; they thought of themselves as supermen, but it was all a mistake. And now we are aweary from our finally successful effort to teach them that the world is a partnership, not a monopoly.

Six years have passed since I last saw London, six of the most eventful years in the history of that hoary capital; we have seen the course of empire take its way westward, and the centre of financial gravity shifted to New York. Shall we take advantage of our opportunities? I fear not. For well over a year we have been like a ship without a rudder, keeping our course only through our own momentum; but we have begun to slow down, and in another year we shall be drifting this way and that with the ebb and flow of the tide; on the rocks perhaps, for since the signing of the Armistice no one has been at the helm of our ship of state. "Ship of state!" Call it rather the "Pinafore," manned by such a crew as has never been seen off the comic-opera stage.

Forty-odd years ago, the exquisite wit of W. S. Gilbert, working in collaboration with that of a gifted musician, Arthur Sullivan, produced one of the most rollicksome, jolliest, and tunefulest of comic operas. It was so merry, and, with all the humor, was so pointed and obvious, that it swept over the entire world. In our own country there was hardly a church choir that was not provided with the words and music, which were sung upon every possible occasion.

Mercifully it is not often that what has served to give one generation exquisite amusement should be seriously adopted by another generation as a form of administration during a great crisis in its history. Perhaps it has never been done before; and the results of so doing have been so disastrous that it may never be done again; but one never can tell — we have such a genius for destruction! Is it not curious that our political rewards go, almost invariably, either to a commonplace man, because he has not made enemies and is for that reason "available," or to one who, ostensibly in the interests of reform, has destroyed something. Our methods of rewards and punishments are so unusual as to excite the remark of other nations. If a man achieves distinction in art or science, he is completely ignored; if he does a fine piece of constructive work, whether in railroading or what not, the government seeks to destroy his work and, whether successful or otherwise, holds up to scorn the man who has created it. Such success as we had in the war was almost entirely due to our business men, whom at one time or another the government sought to destroy.

On the other hand, our politicians, too frequently recruited from our criminal classes, are the raw material out of which our statesmen are made. We are familiar with the legal axiom that "ignorance of the law is no excuse." We might go further and suggest that ignorance is the passport to authority. Certainly it is no bar to high office. We have permitted ourselves to think that the silliest thing in the world is the plot of a comic opera. There is one thing even sillier, and that is the method by which we select, or have selected for us, those who would govern us. Think of the present Mayor of New York City, or the former Director of Public Safety, so-called, of the City of Philadelphia! Is it any wonder that a man well born, well educated, honest and conscientious, shrinks from politics as a career? And we are so complacent at this state of things that those who complain are generally regarded as unpatriotic.

If by chance a man is well equipped for the office he holds, what happens? He looks about him, and too frequently sees his constituents amused by, or indifferent to, his efforts on their behalf. He asks for assistance. Thumbs down!

We are the only nation that keeps, if we may be said to keep, an annual Thanksgiving Day, and we have much to be thankful for: we dwell on a great continent, in the enjoyment of its practically unscratched resources; but politically we are babes in a wood. It would be proper for the nations of Europe to hold an international thanksgiving day, on which all the inhabitants of Britain, Germany, France, Italy, and Russia, in the order named, should drop on their knees and give thanks to their respective gods for our administrative stupidity.[1]

Meanwhile, the Empire upon which the sun never sets is greater than ever. Not long ago I dropped into Drake's bookshop in 40th Street, New York, to pass half an hour while waiting for a friend who was to join me at lunch at my club near-by. I was blue: it seemed as if I owed money to every bookseller in New York, and there had been a five-point decline in United Kingdom bonds in which I had been injudiciously investing.

I had determined to pay my bills and to buy nothing, and was about leaving the shop when Drake said, "There is a little book that you ought to buy; fifty dollars."

I looked at it: Kipling's Poems; but the value was

---

[1] For example, Mr. Wilson, or his advisers, caused two terrific panics — a buying panic and a selling panic — in the sugar trade, to develop in the year 1920. Thousands of business men will carry the marks of this quite unnecessary disaster to their dying day. I am quite sure that my friend Mr. Earl D. Babst, President of the American Sugar Company, will be glad to send to anyone interested the details of this remarkable occurrence.

On the subject of "prohibition" I forbear to speak.

given it by a verse in Kipling's handwriting, signed
by him, reading,—

> If England were what England seems,
> And not the England of our dreams,
> But made of putty, brass and paint,
> How quick we'd chuck her — *But she ain't.*

"No," said I, "I'm not to be tempted." And I
went off to my club, ate my lunch meditatively, and
finally said to myself, "Don't be a fool! Go back and
buy that book."

Lighting a cigar, I strolled slowly back to Drake's
and, as I entered, met him at the door, saying to a
departing customer, "You'll not regret your purchase."

Something told me his customer had the Kipling
(I saw that he had a book under his arm). I stopped
him. "Sir," I said, "is it possible that you have
bought that volume of Kipling with a verse in it?"

"Why, yes," he replied. "Did you want it?"

"I saw it an hour ago, and came back for it," said I.

"Well," said he, "you are too late; to quote your
own words, 'I shall not pass this way again.'" And
he went out wearing as cheery a smile as I have ever
seen on the face of any man.

I often wonder whether the English will ever understand us, or we them; whether the net result of
the war, in so far as a better understanding between
the two nations is concerned, is not to increase rather
than diminish the differences between us. We are so
cocky and vulgar, and they are so condescending and
supercilious.

JAMES F. DRAKE
From an etching by Wall

During all the long weary days of the war I never for a moment doubted that England would dictate the terms of peace; even after we entered and threw our immense resources of men and money into the balance, not even on that dreadful day when Gough's fifth army was destroyed, when Amiens was almost within rifle-shot of the enemy, when Haig made the announcement that would have prostrated any other nation, "Our backs are to the wall," never did it occur to me to doubt that England would dictate the terms of peace; but how completely she would win the war, I began to suspect only when the President made the fatal mistake of going to Paris, there, alone and unaided,— for he would have it so,— to confront the most astute diplomats of the time. Why did he do it? Any tyro could have told him that, if he had kept out of the hurly-burly of Paris he could have imposed his will upon the world. If he had but remained secluded and detached! But his vanity got the upper hand, and he made the fatal mistake of showing Europe that he was not the god it, for a moment, thought him, but a man like other men.

"Politics is adjourned," he cried, meanwhile playing the game more coarsely than it has ever been played before in such a crisis, and flagrantly insulting the men with whom he knew that, sooner or later, he would have to work. The one clear and unequivocal statement that came from Paris was the announcement of the death of Roosevelt, which we knew of before he did, and with the details of which it was absurd for him to clutter up the cables. And so, surrounded by little men,— for he could work with none other,— with whom he quarreled and whom he insulted when they disagreed with him, he played a lone hand, and lost. Perhaps it was well for us that he did. Who knows? Certainly he was elected President of the United States and not President of a League of Nations, to which he had no right to commit us without our consent. The little group of "willful men" in the Senate who opposed him simply insisted upon not being deprived of their constitutional rights.

A considered "Life and Times of Woodrow Wilson" cannot be written in our generation; he has aroused too many antagonisms.

Only when all the actors in the greatest tragedy the world has ever seen are dead, can such a work be attempted. Such books as are now appearing are merely the timber out of which the final story will be constructed. To me the President appears to be cold, selfish, and self-centred, and although fatally fluent in expression, incapable of speaking generously of either friend or foe, or frankly of anything. Unable to make friends,— it would be more exact to say, unable to keep them when made,— he has shown his complete incapacity for working with other men at a time when team-work is a prerequisite for success.

When the old world was in flames, and when it was almost certain that the conflagration would reach these shores, he, in full control of affairs, did not even inquire as to the cost of a chemical engine or order a fire-bucket. When at long last we entered the conflict, it was with a pacifist, who "thanked God that we were unprepared," as Secretary of War, and the editor of a village newspaper as Secretary of the Navy. In our haste we squandered billions. Soon we shall discover that it is easy to borrow but difficult to pay, and our children's children will still be struggling with a burden of debt that his lack of prescience loaded upon us.

Last in the war, Mr. Wilson wills it that we shall be last in peace also — I would not finish the distorted quotation, but rather — "The rest is silence."[1]

[1] In the preparation of these papers for the press, I have allowed my criticism of Mr. Wilson to remain just as it was written a year ago. Occupying for a moment a position exalted beyond his deserts, Mr. Wilson, now a private citizen, may survey that portion of the disaster which, if he did not cause, he could to some extent have prevented. History will for some time be busy with the personality of the man who sought to reverse the old adage, "Actions speak louder than words." While he was "matching minds" with men more flexible and astute than he, the ship of state which he had sworn to protect was pounding upon the rocks. It will be floated after a time by men abler and kindlier than he.

The individual lessens and the world is more and more.

A man may be wiser than some other men, but rarely wiser than all other men. When he feels that he is so, it behooves him to move carefully. To warnings and to danger-signals, Mr. Wilson paid no attention. As the pen-pictures of him multiply, it is seen that the thumb-nail sketch by John M. Keynes, in *The Economic Consequences of the Peace*, is likely to become the official portrait.

VIII

WALT WHITMAN

I WALKED away from Stan. Henkels's auction-room in Walnut Street one afternoon some time ago in a reminiscent mood. Stan. had just "cried the sale," as he calls it, of a lot of Whitman material formerly the property of my old friend, the late Isaac Hull Platt. Dr. Platt has been dead for some years, and in less than two hours a collection had been disposed of which its former owner had spent years in getting together. It is much easier to disperse a collection than to assemble one; I remember how proud Dr. Platt was of his collection, how complete and valuable he thought it. "It will be sold some day," he said, "and it will make the boys sit up." I am glad he was not there; for the boys were not many, and they sat up for a few minutes only and then seemed to fall into a deep sleep, from which the auctioneer roused them with difficulty.

It was not his fault; the fault was with the material, or rather, with the quantity of it. An auction sale, if it is to be successful, must have variety, so that various tastes may be gratified; only when the items are of very great value, can interest in one subject be sustained for several hundred numbers; and so, after a few important first editions and manuscripts had been knocked down at good prices, all enthusiasm

WALT WHITMAN
From a hitherto unpublished photograph

disappeared, and we sat through the sale more from force of habit than anything else.

The time was, in Philadelphia, when anyone of any literary taste whatever affected to know Walt Whitman personally. He was an easy man to know, and commonplace people — and others — buzzed about him like flies and called him "Walt." Much has been written about him; Dr. Platt himself had perpetrated — the word is his own — a short and excellent life of him; and among other such Whitman material, Horace Traubel brought out three volumes of notes, — "Timber," it might well be called,— "With Walt Whitman in Camden," which will be invaluable when the final life of Whitman comes to be written; for we are yet too near him in time, and we in Philadelphia are too near him geographically, to view him in proper perspective. His followers are going rapidly now; Traubel, one of the last and most loyal of them, died only a few weeks ago; and a new generation, which knew not Whitman in the flesh, has hardly yet come into being. For many years he was a picturesque figure in our streets; everyone knew him by sight and regarded him with respectful, if somewhat amused, curiosity.

But he would be a rash prophet who should declare that Whitman is "outmoded," to use a word coined by Max Beerbohm. Rather, he has not yet come into his own. He may yet be regarded in this country as he is in England, as our one great seer. My own guess is that he will be. The voice of a foreigner is the voice of posterity. Listen to what such a one, Holbrook

Jackson,— if an Englishman may be called a foreigner,— says of him : —

"The great poet of the future will neither be classic nor romantic, materialist nor spiritualist. He will have nothing to do with rhymes and metres, or with pretty allusions to mythological gods and goddesses, which have for so long been so great a part of the media of the poets of Europe. All these have the taint of caste and convention, social distinctions, monasticism, and ecclesiasticism, of which Whitman is the direct antithesis. Therefore, he makes his songs akin to the rugged life of America, nearer to earth, nearer to the quickness of things than that of Europe ever can be." And again he says: "If I were asked to name the most national product of American thought, something more national than the Declaration of Independence, more characteristic than Abraham Lincoln, more individual than Emerson, and more Western than Mark Twain, I should name Walt Whitman. Of all American writings, his are the most native."

For myself, so far as I am aware, I have only one prejudice, and that is a lifelong aversion to the nation that attempted the destruction of England, and by so doing committed suicide; to other things I bring an open mind — a small mind if you will, but open. Charles Lamb expressed the same idea in four words: "I have no repugnances." It was, therefore, the lack of repugnance rather than admiration for Walt Whitman which led me to acquiesce when it was suggested that I should assist in an undertaking to commemorate the centenary of his birth. Poetry is, with me, a thing of choice, a luxury rather than a necessity, and I own to a preference for the poetry of Herrick, say, over that of Walt Whitman "sounding his barbaric yawp over the roof of the world," and in America's name "raising high the perpendicular hand" in a *salut au monde*. But I agreed to go along when, after a conference, it was decided that a bronze medal should be cast under the ægis of the Franklin Inn Club of Philadelphia, and that Dr. R. Tait McKenzie should make the design. The medal, a round plaque five inches in diameter, was greatly admired, and the number of subscribers was very gratifying and testified — to what : an increasing interest in Whitman or an appreciation of the work of the medalist? Who shall say?

I received one letter, however, from an old friend, who should have known better than to send me such a communication. His name, which I now withhold, will be sent to the curious upon the payment of a small fee. The letter reads : —

"I have been assaulted with a proposal to subscribe for a medal of that old vulgarian Walt Whitman. It seems to have your name upon it. I shall gladly subscribe to anything that you recommend, but when I think of this old four-flusher and his inconsequential companions, who used to hold forth in the rear of Dooner's saloon, where he always drank and never paid, my heart goes out to you as a generous and Christian gentleman. Personally, I would not give the best line that he wrote house-room in a stable. The medal itself looks like a very genial representation of Boreas, and the artist deserves great credit for making such an attractive affair of such a miserable subject. Yours affectionately."

So it would appear that there are still differences of opinion in regard to Whitman, and it seemed wise for me, as in some measure the sponsor of the Franklin Inn Medal, to brush the dust from my dozen volumes or so of the Good Gray Poet, and reacquaint myself with his work. My opinion of him can be summed up in a sentence. Whitman was a poet only in the sense that he was a prophet. He was a man without taste, and he had no power of selection. He celebrated himself in the first line he ever published, and he continued to do so throughout his life. He has some noble thoughts, but they are thoughts which do not bear transportation; that is to say, they do not pass current. One does not quote Whitman. His admirers speak of him as "spacious." I should rather say, diffuse.

I am reminded of the story of the man who, being asked the name of his favorite poet, replied, "Wordsworth. Wordsworth without a doubt. I keep a volume of him by my bedside and when I am restless and cannot sleep, I take up the 'Excursion' and am soon in a profound slumber." If Whitman's poetry lacks the fine soporific qualities of Wordsworth, it is equally deficient in that exquisite aptness of word and phrase which we so greatly admire in those poets who have so permanently enriched our language. Nor of humor has he a single trace. One could have

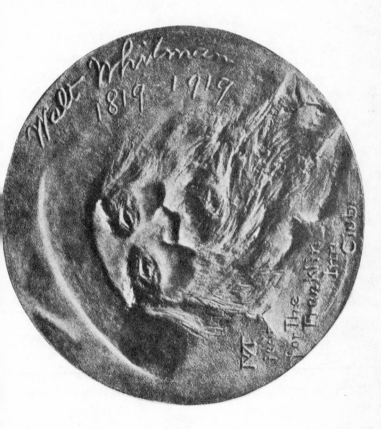

WALT WHITMAN

From a bronze plaque published by the Franklin Inn Club of Philadelphia in honor of his centenary,
— by R. Tait McKenzie

told Whitman that he was greater than Shakespeare and he would have turned never a hair — and he could have turned many. No rhyming dictionary was part of his literary outfit; on the other hand, he must have written with a gazetteer at his elbow. Listen: —

I see the cities of the earth and make myself at random a part of them,
I am a real Parisian,
I am a habitant of Vienna, St. Petersburg, Berlin, Constantinople,
I am of Adelaide, Sydney, Melbourne,
I am of London, Manchester, Bristol, Edinburgh, Limerick,
I am of Madrid, Cadiz, Barcelona, Oporto, Lyons, Brussels, Berne, Frankfort, Stuttgart, Turin, Florence,
I belong in Moscow, Cracow, Warsaw, or northward in Christiania or Stockholm, or in Siberian Irkutsk, or in some street in Iceland,
I descend upon all those cities, and rise from them again.

It reads like an unskillful parody, but it is not; it is genuine Whitman. What he means to say is that he is universal; but think how he has imposed upon the type-setter, to say nothing of the reader.

Whitman during the later years of his life lived in Camden — a depressing city, full of commonplace people whom he affected to love; and only a genius could so write of Camden as to make one wish to go there, even for an hour. It expresses to me our civilization at its very worst. It is an ugly and neglected town, as, unhappily, so many of our towns are. The wretched little house in which Whitman lived, and where he died, 328 Mickel Street, is now a filthy Italian tenement. It is interesting only in Pennell's

charming little etching of it, which George Gras-
burger, the bookseller, generously gave me one day
when I dropped in upon him. I met the poet
several times — once at a meeting of the Contemporary Club, shortly before his death, at which he
read some of his poems; and I went to his funeral,
chiefly because I wanted to hear Robert G. Ingersoll
deliver an oration at his grave, and was much disappointed thereat. Oratory always leaves me cold.
So when Ingersoll summoned "the silent sisters of the
night to draw with rosy fingers the damask curtains
of the dawn," I reached for my hat and crept outside
the tent, which had been erected over the grave in
the event of bad weather. "I felt as if I had been
at the entombment of Christ," wrote one of his dis-
ciples, who attended the funeral. I had no such feeling. Whitman's funeral was a great event in Camden, where little of interest happens. The large tent
and the crowd suggested to me a circus, and this impression was heightened by the general confusion
and by boys in attendance selling peanuts.

Not long before his death, I wrote to him that I
would like to buy several autographed copies of "The
Leaves of Grass," and that I could call for them on
any day and hour he might name. In reply I received a note from him, telling me how to come. I
followed his instructions and received the volumes.
At that time he appeared to be relying upon the sale
of his poems for his livelihood, and the ten dollars I
then spent was, for me, a very considerable sum. I
say "appeared," for, after his death, it developed

WALT WHITMAN'S HOUSE, 328 MICKLE ST., CAMDEN, N. J., IN WHICH HE DIED

From an etching by Joseph Pennell

that, while he was allowing his admirers to pass the hat in his behalf, he was storing up a considerable sum for the handsome and dignified tomb of his own design erected in Harleigh Cemetery.

Until I attended the sale of Dr. Buck's collection, one hundred and forty-seven items in all, I had no idea how extensive the Whitman literature is. I had long wanted a first edition of the "Leaves of Grass"; the centenary of Whitman's birth brought several copies to the surface. Dobell, the English bookseller, catalogued a copy in cloth for eighteen guineas, which I at once cabled for; but the book had been sold by the time my cable arrived. Meanwhile, I had declined a copy offered me by a New York dealer for one hundred and twenty-five dollars. The Buck sale gave me the opportunity I wanted, and I secured a copy.

The story of the publication of the first edition of the "Leaves of Grass" is well told in the admirable reprint, which has just been brought out by Thomas Bird Mosher of Portland, Maine, in which undertaking my friend William Francis Gable of Altoona, Pennsylvania, has had an important part. From him I received a copy with an inscription which makes it very dear to me.

Camerado, this is no book.
Who touches this, touches a man.

Doubtless it is so. His one enduring work is "Leaves of Grass," the first edition of which was published in 1855; and he kept adding to it and subtracting from it — rather adding than subtracting — all his life. If poets—and others—would leave their work alone after they have finished it, the task of the book-collector would be much simplified. With the exception of the first, all the editions of the "Leaves" published during the poet's life-time were both ugly and clumsy. Bliss Perry truly says that the wide page of the first edition gave to Whitman's long lines a dignity not approached in any subsequent issue. This is the edition for which Whitman himself set the type, in the printing-house of the Brothers Rome, in Brooklyn. Neither the name of the author nor that of any publisher is given on the title-page, which reads simply: "Leaves of Grass. Brooklyn, New York: 1855." Opposite the title-page is a steel engraving of the author, and the copyright notice reads, "By Walter Whitman." Its success, or lack of success, was exactly what might have been expected; notwithstanding the fact that the book was freely put out "on sale" and copies sent to all the leading magazines and newspapers, very few were actually sold. In his later days Whitman used to talk of the one man who actually bought a copy of the book, not attempting to reconcile this statement with the one made in his open letter to Emerson, in the second edition, of which he said, "I printed a thousand copies" (of the first edition) "and they readily sold."

Mr. Mosher says, "Of the thousand copies of the 1855 edition, some were given away; most of them were lost, abandoned, or destroyed." The whole edition was not bound at once; those first bound had the words "Leaves of Grass" stamped in gold on both sides and back of the old fashioned dark-green cloth, three gold lines forming a border around the front and back of the cover. Moreover, these had gilt edges, whereas in those subsequently bound the gilt was entirely omitted, except on the front cover; all the rest of the stamping was "blind," and the gilt edges also were omitted, doubtless to save expense. But the important difference between the first and second issue of the first edition is the inclusion in the latter of eight pages of press notices, set in small type in double column — most of them, it is believed, written by the poet himself.

Not discouraged by the failure of the first, Whitman at once proceeded with the publication of a second edition. He had sent Emerson a first edition of the "Leaves," and was much pleased to receive from him a letter in which, among other things, he had said, "I greet you at the beginning of a great career." Whitman had a keen advertising sense in his early days,— indeed, it never deserted him,— and he immediately seized upon these words and stamped them in large letters of gold on the back of his second edition. This somewhat disconcerted the Concord Sage, all the more that the book had upon its first appearance been greeted with a loud chorus of abuse in which the words, "vulgarity," "filth," "muck," "obscenity," "nonsense," etc., were distinctly heard. A few favorable notices, indeed, there were, notably one by Edward Everett Hale; but most of the criticisms, except those which Whitman was accused of writing himself, dealt with the work severely.

If the first edition of the "Leaves" was unusually thin, the second edition, which appeared the year following, was unusually fat and clumsy. It bore, as has been said, by way of a slogan, the sentence from Emerson's letter. It is the cloth binding, therefore, of the second edition, which gives it its value; it is quite as rare as the first, and like that edition, it has no publisher's name, Messrs. Fowler and Wells, "Phrenologists and Publishers," who brought it out, preferring not to have their name associated with the venture, as they had originally intended. Indeed, until quite recently, when Doubleday, Page & Co. took over the copyright of all Whitman's publications, he never had a first-class publisher. Tennyson has been accused of driving a hard bargain with his publishers. Whitman, it may be presumed, did the same. Most of the editions of the "Leaves" are poorly printed on cheap paper, and the price of five dollars for several of them was justified only by the fact that he, as he said, "handled" them himself and autographed them for purchasers. I have several such copies, one as large and clumsy as a good-sized dictionary, another bound in leather, with a pocket and flap, looking for all the world like an engineer's handbook.

Thayer and Eldridge of Boston were the first publishers to put their name to the "Leaves." Their edition, being the third, was published in 1860–61. Shortly afterwards the war broke out, and Whitman disappears; he did not enlist,— "for the eighteen months there is practically no word of him,"—but that he was deeply moved by the struggle between the North and South, we may believe; and we next hear of him in Washington, nursing back to life and health soldiers from either army. Nothing is more beautiful and touching than this episode in Whitman's life; and one of his tiny note-books, which he carried with him when he went about the hospitals as wound-dresser, was sold recently at auction in New York for a high price. Bibliographically, Whitman has not yet come into his own; but he is coming, and there will be great advances in Whitmaniana in the next few years, or my judgment is at fault.

I secured a few months ago a long, clearly written manuscript, signed and dated, in which Whitman gave a succinct account of the Thayer and Eldridge volume. Unlike most of Whitman's manuscripts, it is practically free from erasures and corrections. I believe it has never been printed before, and for this reason I quote it *verbatim*.

Nov. 26, 1880.

R. Worthington, 770 Broadway, New York about a
year ago bo't at auction the electrotype plates (456 pages)
of the 1860 – '61 edition of my book *Leaves of Grass* —
plates originally made by a young firm *Thayer & Eldridge*
under my supervision there and then in Boston, (in the
Spring 1860, on an agreement running five years.) A
small edition was printed and issued at the time, but in
six months or thereabout Thayer & Eldridge failed, and
these plates were stored away and nothing further done
till about a year ago (latter part of 1879) they were put
up in N. Y. City by Leavitt, auctioneer, and bought in
by said Worthington. (Leavitt before putting them up,
wrote to me offering the plates for sale. I wrote back that
said plates were worthless, being superseded by a larger
& different edition — that I could not use them, the 1860
ones, myself, nor would I allow them to be used by any
one else — I being the sole owner of the copyright.)

However, it seems Leavitt did auction them & Worthington bo't them (I suppose for a mere song) — W. then
wrote to me offering $250. if I would add something to the
text & authenticate the plates to be published in a book
by him. I wrote back (I was in St. Louis at the time,
helpless, sick) thanking him for the offer, regretting he had
purchased the plates.

Then & since I thought the matter had dropt. But I
have to add that about September 1880 (I was in London,
Canada at the time) I wrote to Worthington referring to
his previous offer then declined by me, and asking whether
he still had the plates & was disposed to make the same
offer; to which I received no answer. I wrote a second
time; and again no answer.

I supposed the whole thing dropt & nothing done, but
within a week past I learn that Worthington has been
slyly printing and selling the volume of *Leaves of Grass*

from those plates (must have commenced early in 1880)
and is now printing and selling it. On Nov. 22, 1880, I
found the book (printed from those plates) at Porter &
Coates' store, Cor. 9th & Chestnut Sts., Philadelphia.
P & C told me they procured it from Worthington & had
been so procuring it off and on for nearly a year.

First, I want Worthington effectually stopt from issu-
ing the book. Second, I want my royalty for all he has
sold, (though I have no idea of ever getting a cent).
Third, I want W. taken hold of, if possible, on criminal
proceeding.

I am the sole owner of the copyright & I think my copyright papers are all complete — I publish and sell the book
myself — it is my sole means of living — what Worthington has done has already been a serious detriment to me.
Mr. Eldridge (of the Boston firm alluded to) is accessible
in Washington, D. C. — will corroborate first parts of the
foregoing — (is my friend).

WALT WHITMAN, 431 Stevens Street,

Camden, New Jersey.

Later editions are largely without bibliographical
interest; and with the poems that had their origin
in the war and in Lincoln, Whitman's work was done.
His "Specimen Days" and "November Boughs"
and the rest have never found the readers they deserve, except warm admirers and students; they
are, and will probably remain, neglected.

Leaving Washington, he drifted to Camden, where
his mother lived and where she died. After her
death, he "just staid on." The New York "Sun" —
my favorite newspaper — once described Camden as
the refuge of those who were in doubt, debt, or despair. It seems pertinent to ask why Hoboken has

been overlooked? Whitman was not in doubt —
never for a moment: he was a cocksure person; he
was not in debt, his friends saw to that; nor was he
in despair. He "loafed and invited his soul." In
the disorder of his tiny sitting-room in the Mickel
Street house, he received his friends—who were loyal
to him to the last—and in his dogmatic and rather
vulgar way laid down the law to his commonplace
retainers.

One curious incident in his life came fully to light
only when Thomas B. Harned, one of his literary
executors, published a few years ago "The Letters of
Anne Gilchrist to Walt Whitman." They are remarkable not so much for what they reveal as for
what they suggest; indeed, considering the ages and
respective positions of the writer and the recipient,
they are rather bewildering.

Whitman had early found his greatest admirers,
not in the crowded streets of New York and Philadelphia, but in England. It may be that the rough,
the rather uncouth sentiments of democracy acted
like a tonic upon those accustomed to the somewhat
vitiated atmosphere of London drawing-rooms and
Chelsea studios. Indeed, if the beauty of anything
is increased by distance, democracy is that thing.
Swinburne and the two Rossettis early professed
allegiance to Whitman, and through them and Madox
Brown, Mrs. Gilchrist became acquainted with his
work. William Michael Rossetti had selected and
edited an edition of the "Leaves," and to him she
writes: "Since I have had it, I can read no other

book; it holds me entirely spellbound, and I go through it again and again with deepening delight and wonder."

To which Rossetti replies: "That glorious man, Walt Whitman, will one day be known as one of the greatest of the sons of earth, a few steps below Shakespeare on the throne of immortality."

Mrs. Gilchrist was a widow of mature years, the mother of four children, when she fell under the spell of Whitman's verbal fascination. Perhaps more than anyone else, she, in her "Estimate of Walt Whitman," — and an excellent and judicial estimate it is,— printed in the "Radical" for May, 1870, voiced the belief generally held in England as to the value of his work. Praise was ever sweet to Whitman; it could not be too sweet. Few souls have the rugged strength of character of Sam Johnson, who once said to a lady who was buttering him, "Consider, madame, what your flattery is worth before you choke me to death with it." The correspondence, which began as a result of her public appreciation of Whitman, continued to grow more personal and impassioned until, in spite of his efforts to prevent it, Mrs. Gilchrist announced that she was coming to this country, in order that she might be near the object of her passion. It was her wish to be "full of sweet comfort to her beloved's soul and body through life, through and after death." "I do not approve!" screamed Whitman across the Atlantic; but to no avail; and the lady, being then a grandmother and approaching her fiftieth year, with her household impedimenta and several children, took passage for Philadelphia on August 30, 1876.

It was the year of the Centennial Exposition, and Philadelphia was overcrowded and was experiencing such heat as is unusual even in our torrid town. Nevertheless, the lady came and stayed. For almost two years, from a commonplace house in a commonplace section of our city, 1929 North Twenty-second Street, the lady besought the poet unsuccessfully. She then raised the siege and, after a little, sailed away.

Whitman carried himself through this trying ordeal rather as a gentleman than as a poet; undoubtedly age had something to do with it. He was growing old, was in poor health, and in no humor to take part in such an intrigue as would have delighted him at an earlier period in his career. He became a courteous, constant, and attentive visitor at Mrs. Gilchrist's house, and her affection for and interest in him did not lessen with propinquity. Her letters to him after their parting are respectful and affectionate. When, after her death, her son Herbert, while preparing the biography of his mother, asked to see the letters, Whitman with proper delicacy declined. He said: "I do not know that I can furnish any good reason, but I feel to keep these utterances exclusively to myself; but I cannot let your book go to press without at least saying and wishing to put it on record that, among the perfect women I have met, I have known none more perfect in every relation than my dear, dear friend, Anne Gilchrist."

THE TOMB OF WALT WHITMAN IN HARLEIGH CEMETERY

I owe this beautiful picture to the courtesy of William C. Jones, Esq., of Camden, N. J., who had the photograph made for me.   A.E.N.

I wish that he had destroyed the letters.   Someone
has said that biographies are of three sorts: biographies, autobiographies, and ought-not-to-be-ogra-
phies. Love-letters it seems to me are of this latter
kind. Only when they are as wonderful and beautiful as those of Heloise to Abelard, and when they
have been purified, as it were, by time, can they be
read without a pitying or a scornful smile. I once,
years ago and absentmindedly, dropped into a letter-
box a railway ticket and my sleeping-car reservation
for Chicago, and later sought to board my train with
a love-letter as my passport. I learned something
at that time which has been of use to me since.

From contemplation one may become wise, but
knowledge comes only by study. It was the future
rather than the past that interested Whitman, and
he prophesied in a large and ample way, carefully
avoiding details. The names of the world's great
men came glibly to his tongue as needed, but I
suspect that he knew little of them besides. His
literary judgments and pronouncements were frequently foolish. Listen to this nugget of criticism
which especially offends me: "We are no admirer of
such characters as Dr. Johnson. He was a sour,
malicious, egotistical man. He was a sycophant of
power and rank, withal; his biographer narrates that
he 'always spoke with rough contempt of popular
liberty.' His head was educated to the point of plus;
but for his heart might still more unquestionably
stand the sign minus. He insulted his equals . . .
and tyrannized over his inferiors. He fawned upon

his superiors, and, of course, loved to be fawned upon himself. . . . Nor were the freaks of this man the mere 'eccentricities of genius'; they were probably the faults of a vile, low nature. His soul was a bad one."

As has been truly said, Whitman requires to be forgiven more generously than any other great writer. He does, indeed.

Whitman had his Boswell in the person of Horace Traubel, whom we all greatly respected and admired. Traubel had at least a trace of what Whitman lacked entirely, namely, a sense of humor. I once called him an inspired lead-pencil and he took no offense; nor was any intended; I had in mind his biographical work, "With Walt Whitman in Camden," rather than his poems (?) in his "Conservator." I remember that he used to publish at the head of one of his columns in that paper a criticism: "Horace is certainly a lovely fellow; but there is no use talking, he writes rotten poetry." I entirely agree. Traubel's devotion to his hero much resembled Boswell's to Johnson. This misled people into likening Whitman to the great Cham of Literature, whom he resembled just as little as Camden resembles London. Dr. Johnson was the intimate friend of the most distinguished men and women of his time. In the greatest city of the world he was its dominating literary figure.

From time to time Whitman had important visitors from abroad, but distinguished men and women in this country left him largely alone. When the second centenary of his birth rolls around, I venture to prophesy that Whitman will be more truly honored than he was at the meeting at the Elks' Hall in Camden on the one hundredth anniversary of his birth.

IX

"20"

WE were in London,— a maiden uncle and a presumably maiden aunt and I,— and I was showing my relatives the town, which I knew well, with a fine air of proprietorship. It happened years ago. There were omnibuses in those days — not huge, self-propelled motor-busses, driven at a breakneck pace through the crowded streets, but gayly painted, lazy, rotund coaches, like huge beetles, driven by men who bore a strong family resemblance to the elder Weller. With my party I had been climbing from the top of a bus going east to the top of another going west, when the suggestion was made that the next sight should be a bit of the roast beef of Old England. We were for a moment off the beaten track of the busses, and the only vehicle in sight was a disreputable-looking four-wheel cab, usually denominated a "growler," no doubt from the character of the driver. Rather against my judgment, we entered it and I gave the order, "Simpson's, in the Strand." The driver roused himself and his beast, and we started; but we had gone only a short distance when, in some inexplicable way, the man, who was subsequently discovered to be drunk, locked the wheels of the cab in attempting to make a sharp turn, and completely upset the ramshackle vehicle. Within, there was

A LONDON "GROWLER," DISSATISFIED WITH HIS FARE

From a water-color in the possession of the author

great confusion. Just how it happened I never knew, but in some way my foot got outside the broken window; the horse moved; I heard something snap, felt a sharp pain, and knew that my leg was broken.

A crowd gathered, but the omnipresent policeman was on the spot in a moment, and order was quickly brought out of confusion. My companions were unhurt, but it was instantly realized that I was in real trouble. More policemen arrived, numbers were taken, explanations demanded and attempted; but accidents happen in the crowded streets of London at the rate of one a minute or so, and the rules are well understood. A shrill blast on a whistle brought several hansoms dashing to the scene. I had become the property of the Corporation of the City of London in general, and of St. Bartholomew's Hospital in particular. The custom is, when one is hurt in the streets of London, that he is taken at once to the nearest hospital. His not to reason why: "it's an 'ard, faast rule."

Fortunately, the hospital was near at hand, and in a very few moments, I found myself lying on a bench in the casualty ward, writhing in agony, and surrounded by a crowd of young men curious to know how it happened. The general opinion, as voiced by a young cockney, who seemed to be in authority, was that I had had a "naasty one," and that Mr. Peterson would probably "take it hoff at the knee." It was my intention to expostulate with Mr. Peterson when he arrived and I hoped he would come quickly; but when he appeared, he seemed so intelligent and

sympathetic, that I indulged myself in the hope that
I and "it" would be safe in his hands.   The entrance
of a seriously injured man into a London hospital
confers no distinction upon him — he is regarded, not
as an individual, but simply as another casualty,
making six, or sixteen, taken to the operating room
that morning.   My arrival, therefore, was taken
quite as a matter of course.   A few questions were
asked by a recorder, and as soon as I had told him
who I was, where I lived, my age and best friend, I
was picked up, placed upon a stretcher, and carried
away, I knew not whither.

Within the hospital there was neither surprise,
confusion, nor delay.   They might have been expecting me.   Almost before I knew it, I was being rapidly
but skillfully undressed.   I say undressed, but in
point of fact my trousers and one shoe were being
removed, with the aid of several pairs of shears in
skillful hands.   I was curious to see for myself the
extent of the injury that seemed so interesting to
those about me, but this was not permitted.   Someone ventured the opinion, for which I thanked him,
that as I was young and clean, I had more than an
even chance to save my leg; another remarked that
there was no place in the world like "Bart's," for
fractures, and that with luck my wound might begin
to heal "by first intention."

Meanwhile I divined rather than saw that prep-
arations for a serious operation were under way.
Nurses with ominous-looking instruments wrapped
up in towels made their appearance, and I heard the

word "chloroform" used several times; then a rubber
pad was put over my face, I felt someone fumbling
at my wrist and I was told to take a deep breath. In
a moment I was overcome by a sickening sensation
occasioned by something sweetish; I felt lifted
higher, higher, higher — until suddenly something
seemed to snap in my head, and I awoke, in exquisite pain and very sick at the stomach.

Several hours had elapsed; I found myself quite
undressed and in a bed in a large room in which were
many other beds similar to mine, most of them occupied. Leaning over me was a white-capped nurse,
and at the foot of the bed was a very kindly-looking
woman, a lady of mature years, wearing an elaborate
cap, whom I heard addressed as "Sister." I had
lost my identity and had become merely "20," Pitcairn Ward, St. Bartholomew's Hospital, London —
one of the oldest and, as I was to discover, one of the
best hospitals in the world.

I was in great agony and very lonely. Things had
happened with such rapidity that I could scarcely
realize how I came to be where I was. I inquired
for my relatives, and was told that they would "be
here presently." I asked for Dr. Peterson, and was
told that he, too, would be here "presently." From
the pain I felt I made no doubt that he had after all
taken "it" off at the knee, as prophesied.

"Presently" I heard outside the door a great
scuffling of feet, as of the approach of a considerable
crowd; then the door opened and there entered a
group of students, led by an elderly and distinguished-

looking man who, visiting a row of cots in turn,
finally came to mine and, without speaking to me,
took my chart from a nurse and studied it attentively.
A moment later Mr. Peterson came up and explained
what he had done, to all of which the distinguished
man, addressed as Mr. Willett, listened attentively,
expressing his satisfaction and saying "exactly"
several times.

Finally, Mr. Willett addressed the crowd gathered
in a semi-circle about my bed. "The patient is suffering from a compound comminuted fracture of the
tibia and fibula; he was fished out of an overturned
four-wheeler just by the Charterhouse Gate. Mr.
Peterson has just performed an operation. He has
—" Here followed a rapid and technical account of
what had been done to me,— and it seemed ample,—
what complications might ensue, and what was hoped
for, ending with congratulations to Mr. Peterson on
having done a very good job. "Six hundred yards
of plaster bandage, eh? good, very good."

I was in great pain and too ill to listen with much
attention to what more he said. At last, as an after-
thought, Mr. Willett again took the chart from the
nurse and, glancing at it indifferently for a moment,
said, "Ah, an American, eh?" Then, turning to me
he added, "They've brought you to the right shop
for fractures, my lad; there's no place in the world
where you would be better off than just where you
are, and Mr. Peterson has made as clean a job as the
best surgeon in"— glancing at the chart again —
"Philadelphia could have done."

"But, doctor," I piped (I did not then know that surgeons in England are always addressed as Mister), "it's not to be forgotten that Dr. Peterson has been working on excellent American material."

Mr. Willett almost dropped the chart in amazement and Sister told me to "Sh-h, don't talk back." Such a thing was unheard of, for a poor devil lying on a cot in a great charity hospital of London to bandy words with one of the greatest surgeons in England. Mr. Willett was too surprised to say anything; he simply turned on his heel and walked away, followed by his students and the Sister, leaving the nurse to tell me that I must never, never talk back to Mr. Willett again. "He's never to be spoke to 'nless he aasks a question."

At half-past five supper was served. I didn't get any, didn't want any. By eight o'clock we were being prepared for the night. How I dreaded it! We were a lot of poor, forlorn men and boys, twenty-four of us, all more or less broken somewhere, all suffering; some groaning and complaining, some silently bearing their agony. In the cot next to mine there was a great burly fellow, who called me Matey and said I was in luck. I didn't care much to pursue the subject, but asked him how he made that out.

"You've had one leg broke twice Hi 'ear: that haain't nuthin'. Hi've 'ad both legs hoff at the knee, and Hi've a missus and six kiddies."

I was inclined to agree with him; but a Susan-Nipper-like person said, "No talking," and I was glad she did.

The pain was dreadful. I wanted a great many little attentions, and got them, from a nurse whose name after all these years I here record with respect and affection — Nurse Hare. Midnight came; I was suffering terribly. Finally I asked Nurse if I could not have a hypodermic. She said she thought I could, and presently came and jabbed a little needle into my arm, at the same time telling me to be very quiet in order that the drug might take effect. At last, I fell into a troubled sleep, only to start out of it again. Still, I got a little sleep from time to time, and finally morning came. A few days later, when Nurse Hare and I were exchanging confidences, she told me the hypodermic was of cold water only. "I could n't 'ave given you a 'ypodermic without orders," she said.

Morning comes slowly in London; sometimes in December it can hardly be said to come at all; but breakfast comes. By six o'clock the gas was lit, and hot water and basins and towels were passed about to those who could use them. Confusion took the place of comparative quiet. I had not tasted food for almost twenty-four hours. I was hungry. The pain in my leg was a deep throbbing pain, but it could be borne. I began to look about me. Some-one said, "Good-morning, Twenty," and I replied, "Good-morning, Seventeen. What kind of a night did you have?" — "Rotten, 'ad the 'ump." It occurred to me that I had always wanted to talk to a pure and undefiled cockney and that I now had an excellent opportunity to learn. Breakfast, which

SMITHFIELD ENTRANCE TO SAINT BARTHOLOMEW'S HOSPITAL

came to me on a tray, was delicious: porridge and milk, tea, bread, butter, and jam. I wanted a second round, but something was said about temperature, and I was forced to be content.

Late in the day, as it seemed, but actually about nine o'clock, my uncle came to see me. Poor fellow, he too had passed a sleepless night and showed it. What could he do for me? There was just one man I wanted to see above all others — my friend Hutt, or as he pronounced it, 'Utt, the bookseller in Clements Inn Passage. Would my uncle go and bring him to me? He would; he did not say so, but he would have fetched me a toothpick from the furtherest inch of Asia if I had asked for it. He had never seen Mr. Hutt, he had been in London only some forty-eight hours, he did not know his way around, and was as nervous as a hen. I told him as well as I could where Hutt's shop was and he started off; as he went, I noticed he was carrying my umbrella, which had a rather curious horn handle studded with round-headed silver tacks — quite an unusual-looking handle. I am telling the exact truth when I say that my uncle promptly lost his way, and an hour later, my friend Hutt, hurrying along the crowded Strand, saw a man wandering about, apparently looking for someone or something, *and carrying my umbrella*. He went up and, calling my uncle by name (he had heard me speak of him), asked if he could direct him anywhere. My uncle was amazed, as well he might be, and conducted my friend, or rather was conducted by him, to my bedside.

When Mr. Willett came in on his rounds later in the day, my uncle entered upon a rather acrimonious discussion with him on the subject of my being a charity patient in a public ward. Mr. Willett explained very patiently that I should have every attention, but as for private rooms, there were none. Whatever I needed, the hospital would supply, but under the rules nothing could be brought in to me, nothing of any kind or character, and no tips or fees were permitted. Finally my uncle, dear old man, broke down and cried; and then Mr. Willett, like the gentleman he was, said, "I tell you what I'll do. There are no private rooms, but so sure I am that your nephew would not in a week's time go into one if there were, that I promise that, when he can be moved without danger, I will personally put him in a nursing home and take care of him myself if he wishes it; but I know from experience that your nephew will find so much of interest going on about him that he will wish to remain here. We have had gentlemen here before — why, sir, nobility even."

With this we were forced to be content, and it turned out exactly as Mr. Willett prophesied.

My greatest discomfort arose from my being compelled to remain always in one position. With my leg in a plaster-cast, in which were two windows through which my wounds were observed and dressed, and securely fastened in a cradle, I was compelled to remain on my back and could move only my upper body without assistance. At first I found this desperately irksome, but I gradually became accustomed to it. I was greatly helped by a simple device which I thought at the time a great blessing; I have never seen it elsewhere, and wonder why. In the wall about eight feet above the head of each bed was set a stout iron bracket, a bracket strong enough to bear the weight of a heavy man. From the end of the bracket, about thirty inches from the wall, hung a rope, perhaps five feet long; a handle-bar with a hole in it, through which the rope passed, enabled one to adjust the handle at any height desired above the bed. A knot at the end of the rope prevented the handle slipping off and fixed the lower limit of its travel, but it could be adjusted by another knot at any higher point desired. The primary object of this device, which was called a pulley, was to enable the patient to lift himself up in bed without subjecting his lower body to strain of any kind. But it had many other purposes. From it one could hang one's newspaper, or watch, or handkerchief, and it served also as a harmless plaything. Have you seen a kitten play with a ball of wool? In like manner have I seen great men relieve the monotony with their pulley, spinning it, swinging it, sliding the handle up and down, for hours at a time.

Without suggesting that I was in any way a conspicuous person in the ward, I am bound to say that my fellow patients treated me as a "toff" — in other words, a swell. This was due solely to the fact that I had a watch. Such a possession in a public ward of a London hospital is like keeping a carriage or a gig; to use Carlyle's word, it is a mark of respectability.

Frequently during the night I would hear some poor
helpless sufferer say, "Hi siay, 20, wot time his hit?"
It occurred to me that it would be a nice thing to have
one of my friends go to Sir John Bennett's, the famous
clockmaker, and buy a small clock with a very soft
strike, which would mark the hours without disturbing anyone. I spoke to Nurse Hare about it, and she
to someone in authority. The answer came: no gifts
could be accepted while I was in the hospital. After
my discharge any gifts I might see fit to make should
be sent to the hospital, to be used as the authorities
thought best, and not to any ward in particular.
Another "'ard, faast rule," and a good one.

Before a week had passed, Christmas was upon us.
The afternoon before, I sent out for a copy of "The
Christmas Carol," which I had read so often before,
and have read so often since, on Christmas Eve.
Through this little book Dickens has, more than any
other man, given Christmas its character of cheer and
good-will; but it reads better in London than elsewhere.

"How's the weather outside?" I asked, looking up
from my book, of a "dresser" who had just come in.

"There's snow on the ground and a regular 'London particular' [fog], and it's beginning to sleet."

I thanked my lucky stars that I was in bed, as
warm as toast, and wondered what I would get for a
"Christmas box,"—that is to say, a Christmas pres-
ent,—for we were all looking forward to something.
There was to be a tree in the adjoining ward, but, as
I could not be moved, I was to have my presents

brought to me. I can still see the gifts I received from
kindly disposed ladies! Useful gifts! A little game of
cards played with Scripture texts; a handkerchief
primarily intended for mental stimulation, with the
alphabet and numbers up to ten printed thereon; a
pair of socks, hand-knitted, of a yarn of the consist-
ency of coarse twine; a pair of pulse-warmers, and a
book,— a copy of "The British Workman,"— and
last, but not least, a pair of stout hobnailed shoes.
Ladies, too, came and offered to read to me, assuming that I could not read to myself, and in other ways
showed their kindness of heart. God bless them every
one.

No one ever worked harder at a foreign language
than I did at learning cockney. I drawled my *o*'s and
i's, and broadened my *a*'s, and dropped my *h*'s and
picked 'em up again and put them in the wrong
place; and I had the best instructors in London. A
few in the ward could read, but more could not; and
almost without exception they spoke that peculiar
dialect which is the curious inheritance of the Londoner. Those of us whose memories go back twenty-
five years or so remember it as the medium of that
great music-hall artist, Albert Chevalier. His songs
were then all the rage, as were, too, Gus Ellen's. As
we became better acquainted, we sang them together,
and I then acquired an accomplishment which has
even yet not entirely deserted me. (I should have
said that it was the custom for the surgical wards of
St. Bartholomew's Hospital to take in accident cases
continuously until all the beds were full; as a result,

most of the patients entered about the same time,
and we came to know one another, by number, very
intimately in the two or four or six weeks' residence.)

Mr. Willett was quite right : I would not have been
moved into a private room for something handsome.
There were so many men worse off than myself, that
I forgot myself in thinking of others. "Twenty-one"
had lost both feet; I certainly was fortunate compared with him. "Seventeen," while cleaning a plate-
glass window from a ladder, had slipped and plunged
through the window, damaging himself horribly in
half a dozen ways; I certainly was lucky compared
with him. "Eight" had undergone three serious op-
erations and another one was contemplated. In
short, as soon as I became reasonably comfortable I
began to feel quite at home. I had my books and
papers and magazines, and spent hours in playing
checkers for a penny a game with a poor chap who
had lost an arm. He almost always beat me, but a
shilling was not much to pay for an afternoon's
diversion.

No one could spend two months or so in St. Bartholomew's Hospital,—"Bart's," as it is affectionately called,— without seeking to know something of
its history. Its origin is shrouded in antiquity. In the
church of St. Bartholomew the Great, wedged into a
corner of Smithfield just outside the gate, is the tomb
of its founder, Rahere, a minstrel, or court jester,
of Henry I. While on a pilgrimage to Rome, he was
stricken with a serious illness, during which he made
a vow that, if he lived to get back to London, he

TOMB OF RAHERE, THE FOUNDER OF ST. BARTHOLOMEW'S HOSPITAL : ONE OF
THE OLDEST MONUMENTS IN LONDON

would build a hospital in thanksgiving. Thus it was
that, in the year 1102, a priory and hospital were
founded. Thanks to the protests of the citizens of London, it not only escaped the attentions of Henry
VIII, when he entered upon his period of destruction, but it was even said to have been reëstablished
by him. Thenceforth it came to be regarded as the
first of royal hospitals. In receipt of a princely income,
it has from time out of mind been the scene of great
events in surgical and medical science. Harvey, physician of Charles I, the discoverer of the circulation
of the blood, was chief physician of the hospital for
more than thirty years. A roll of the distinguished
names would be tedious; but Mr. Willett was quite
right when he said that I had come to the right shop
for fractures. "We make a specialty of fractures"
might have been adopted as a slogan, had slogans
been in vogue when the famous surgeon, Percival Pott,
was thrown from his horse and sustained a compound fracture, and with difficulty prevented a
brother surgeon from giving him first aid with a knife
and saw. How he directed the treatment of his own
case and saved his leg is one of the many legends of
the place.

But to return to Pitcairn Ward. It was a large
room, with a high ceiling, and with two rows of beds,
twelve to a row, on either side of a wide aisle. It was
heated by a soft-coal-burning device, something like
a range, but with a large open grate, the smoke from
which curled lazily up the chimney. One morning it
was discovered that the fire was out; and as this

seemed to indicate neglect, and certainly meant work for the ward-maid, each patient as he woke and made this discovery sang out cheerily, "Fire's out." To these remarks the maid usually replied by asking the speaker to mind his own business; or perhaps she contented herself by making faces or sticking her tongue out at him.

Presently a curious sound was heard from the chimney, as of a fluttering of birds, followed by a curious cry, "Peep, peep, peep," which was instantly recognized by those familiar with it as being the professional call of the chimney sweep. Someone cried, "Sweeps!" The effect was instantaneous. As when one discovers a ship in mid-ocean and announces the fact, all rush to the rail, so all who could crowded in wheel-chairs around the fireplace, only to be told to "Be hoff" by the ward-maid.

Presently the sounds grew louder, until, at last, a tall, slender lad, black with soot from head to foot, armed with brushes and brooms, slid down into the grate, leaped out, gave a little scream, bowed, and disappeared, almost before we could clap our eyes upon him. My intention had been to ask the little urchin to get into a bed next to mine, at that moment vacant, and give an imitation of Charles Lamb's chimney-sweep "asleep like a young Howard in the state bed of Arundel Castle." I probably saved myself a lot of trouble by being so surprised at his quick entrance and get-away that I said not a single word. "A chimney-sweeper quickly makes his way through a crowd by being dirty."

Anything kinder, anything more considerate than
the authorities of the hospital, from Mr. Willett down
to the ward-maid, could hardly be imagined. There
was, however, one ordeal against which I set my face
like flint — namely, shaving. Shaving was I think an
extra; its cost, a penny. Every day a man and a boy
entered the ward, the boy carrying a small tub filled
with thick soapsuds, the man with a razor incredibly
sharp. One cried, "Shaves?" and perhaps from two
or half a dozen beds came the word, "Yus." No time
was lost in preliminaries. A common towel was tied
around one's neck, and a brush like a large round
paint-brush was dipped into the thick lather. With
a quick movement, the result of much practice, the
boy made a pass or two from ear to ear; with a twist
and a return movement, the cheeks, lips, mouth, and
chin were covered with soap. The man wielded a
razor in much the same manner, and the victim spent
the next hour or two patting his face with his hands,
then withdrawing them and looking at them, as if he
expected to see them covered with blood. The operation was complete. I use the word "operation" ad-
visedly; although chloroform was not administered,
I always insisted that it should have been. The first
surgeons were barbers; at least the two trades were
closely allied, and in England they seem to be allied
still. Thanks to the kindness of one of the "dressers,"
when I became well enough to be shaved, I had a real
barber in from a near-by shop. It cost me half a crown,
and was a prolonged agony rather than a brief one;
that was the chief difference; in essentials the opera-

tion was the same. Is it surprising that in England gentlemen invariably shave themselves?

Some men make excellent patients, I am told, when they are very ill, and allow their bad traits to come to the surface as they become convalescent. It was so in my case. I grew tired of the life and began inquiring how much longer my leg was to be kept in plaster. Fortunately I had no idea of the ordeal of removing a plaster-cast which reached from one's toes to one's hip. At last the day came, and I shall never forget it. I had first been permitted to limp around the ward on crutches for a few days, and soon learned to manage them very nicely; and when a time was set for my leg to come out of plaster, I was very thankful. It was the work of hours: every tiny hair on my leg was firmly set in plaster of Paris, and the removal of the cast occasioned such continuous pain that several times I thought I should faint. At last, however, the task was accomplished and I looked down at the leg which had been the subject of so much discussion, which had been dressed so often. It was a poor thing, but mine own; no one else would have had it; a poor, shrunken, shortened, emaciated member, but whole, thank God! I did not then know that a year after the accident happened I should be walking as well as ever; and let me say that I have never had a twinge of pain in it since. Mr. Willett and Mr. Peterson, and "Sister" and Nurse Hare, I doff my hat to you.

Measurements were taken for a leather stocking, which was a work of art; and finally a date was set for my dismissal. A room had been secured for me in a not-distant lodging; for I still had to go to the hospital once or twice a week to have the rapidly healing wounds dressed. I made my departure from the hospital early one afternoon, in what was called a private ambulance; but I am certain that the vehicle was usually used as a hearse. The stretcher on which I was laid was on casters and was pushed into the rear door of a long low contrivance with glass sides. As we prepared to drive away from the hospital gate, an effigy, that of Henry, the Eighth of that name, looked down upon me from his niche over Smithfield Gate. A crowd gathered, and from my horizontal position the unusual sight of so many people moving about in perpendicular made me dizzy. I closed my eyes and heard someone inquire, "Is he dead?" I was very unhappy, and still more so when, half an hour later, I found myself in a very tiny bedroom, as it seemed to me, and in *a bed with no pulley*. I could have cried; indeed, I think I did. I wanted to go back to the hospital; I felt that I was being neglected and should die of suffocation.

A maid came in and asked if I wanted anything. "Want anything!" I certainly did, and I gave her a list of things I wanted, in the most approved cockney. As she left my room, I heard her say to another maid just outside the door, "'Ave you 'eard that bloke hin there talk? Faancy 'im tryin' to paass hisself hoff has comin' from New York!"

X

LIVING TWENTY-FIVE HOURS A DAY

IF one elects to live well out in the country, going to the opera presents serious difficulties. One can't very well go home to dress and go in town again; and if one decides to stay in town at a hotel, there is a suitcase to be packed in the morning — an operation the result of which I abhor, as I always forget something essential. On one occasion, some years ago, I, like a dutiful husband, had agreed to go to the opera, and having packed my bag and sent it to my hotel, dismissed from my mind the details of my toilet, until I came to dress in the evening; when I discovered to my horror that I had absentmindedly packed a colored negligé shirt instead of the white, hard-boiled article which custom has decreed for such occasions, and that several other little essentials were missing. I was quite undressed when I made this discovery; it was already late, and my temper, never absolutely flawless on opera nights, was not improved by my wife's observation that we would surely miss the overture. I thought it altogether likely, and said so — briefly.

It was, as I remember, my Lord Chesterfield who observed that when one goes to the opera one should leave one's mind at home; I had gone his Lordship one better, I had left practically everything at home, and I heartily wished that I was at home, too. I shall not, I think, be accused of misstatement when I say that it is altogether probable that most married men, if they could be excused from escorting their wives to the opera, would cheerfully make a substantial contribution to any worthy — or even unworthy — charity.

Thoughts such as these, if thoughts they may be called, surged through my head, as I rapidly dressed and prepared to dash through the streets in search of any "gents' furnishing goods" shop that might chance to be open at that hour. I needed such articles of commerce as would enable me to make myself presentable at the opera, and I needed them at once. It was raining, and as I dashed up one street and down another, I discovered that the difference between a raised umbrella and a parachute is negligible; so I closed mine, with the result that I was thoroughly drenched before I had secured what I needed. I have the best of wives, but truth compels me to say that when, upon my return, she greeted me with the remark that what she wanted especially to hear was the overture and that we would certainly be late, I almost — I say I *almost* — lost my temper.

Is it necessary for me to remark that we do not go to the opera frequently? It was my wife's evening, not mine; and as I sat on the side of a bed, eating a sandwich and struggling to insert square shirt pegs in round holes, to the gently sustained *motif* that we would surely miss the overture, I thought of home, of my books, of a fire of logs crackling, of my pipe, and

I wondered who it was who said, when anything untoward happened, "All this could have been avoided if I had staid at home."

Finally, after doing up my wife's back,— "hooking them in the lace," — I finished my own unsatisfactory toilet, feeling, and doubtless looking, very much as Joe Gargery did when he went to see Miss Havisham. But at last we were ready, and we descended to the lobby of our hotel, having in the confusion quite overlooked the fact that we should require a taxi. It was still raining, and not a taxi or other conveyance was to be had! I was quite nonplussed for the moment, and felt deeply grieved when my wife remarked that it was hardly worth while now to leave the hotel — we were so late that we should miss the overture anyway; to which I replied — but never mind specifically what I said; it was to the effect that we would go to the opera or bust.

But how? Standing at the door of the hotel, I waited my chance, and finally a taxi arrived; but quite unexpectedly a man appeared from nowhere and was about to enter it, saying, as he did so, in a fine rolling English voice, "I wish to go to the opera house."

There was no time to lose; quickly brushing the man aside, I called to my wife and passed her into the taxi, and then, turning to the stranger, I explained to him that we, too, were going to the opera and that he was to be our guest. I pushed the astonished man into the machine, told the driver to go like h— (to drive rapidly), and entering myself, pulled to the door and heaved a sigh of relief. We were off.

For a moment nothing was said. We were all more or less surprised to find ourselves together. I think I may say that my newly discovered friend was astonished. Something had to be said, and it was up to me to say it. "My name is Newton," I said; and gently waving toward Mrs. Newton a white-kid-gloved hand, which in the darkness looked like a small ham, I explained that Mrs. Newton was very musical and was particularly anxious to hear the overture of the opera, and that I was unavoidably late. I added that I hoped he would forgive my rudeness; then, remembering that I was speaking to an English gentleman who probably thought me mad, I inquired if he were not a stranger in Philadelphia.

"Yes," he replied; "I only arrived in the city this evening."

"And have you friends here?" I asked.

His reply almost disconcerted me: "Present company excepted, none."

"Oh, come now," I said; "I took you for an Englishman, but no Englishman could possibly make so graceful a speech on such short notice. You must be either Scotch or Irish; whenever one meets a particularly charming Englishman, he invariably turns out to be Scotch — or Irish."

"Well, the fact is, I'm Scotch," my friend replied; "my name is Craig, Frank Craig. I'm an artist."

"Don't apologize," I said; "you are probably not a very great artist. I'm a business man, and not a

very great business man either; and as we are the
only friends you have in the city, you shall have
supper with us after the opera. Don't decline. I'm
very much at home in our hotel, as perhaps you noticed. Ask for me at the door of the supper-room.
Don't forget my name. Here we are at the opera
house, in good time for the overture, after all."

And I passed my friend out of the taxi, and he,
assuring me that he would join us at supper, went his
way and we ours.

During the performance, which was miserable, I
chuckled gently to myself, and wondered what my
Scotch friend thought of the affair and whether he
would keep his appointment. The opera was late,
there was the usual delay in getting away, and it was
almost midnight when the head waiter conducted my
new-found guest to our table. Then for the first time
we had a good look at each other, and told each other
how funny it all was, and how unexpected and delightful. After an excellent supper and a bottle of
champagne, followed by a fine brandy and cigars,—
for I determined to do the thing well,— we grew
confidential. We talked of life and of travel, and
finally, of course, about books and authors.

"Have you ever met Booth Tarkington?" my
friend inquired. I had. Did I know him? I did not.
Craig had been staying with him in Indianapolis.
Had I ever heard of Arnold Bennett? I had. Did I
care for his books? I did. He also had been staying
with Booth Tarkington in Indianapolis; in fact,
Bennett and he were traveling together at the pres-

ent time. "Bennett is doing a book for the Harpers,
to be called 'Your United States,'" Craig explained,
and he, Craig, was doing the illustrations for it.

"And where is Arnold Bennett now?" I asked.

"Upstairs, in bed and asleep, I hope."

"What are you doing to-morrow?"

"Well, Bennett is lunching with the literati of the
city, and I'm going to take photographs and make
sketches for our book; we are each on our own, you
know."

"But the literati of the city," I repeated doubt-
fully; "that would be Agnes Repplier, of course, and
Dr. Furness, and Weir Mitchell, and who else?" We
were rather shy of literati at the moment, as we still
are, and I hoped these would not fail him.

Craig did n't know; he had not been invited.

"And after the luncheon, what next?" I inquired.

"Well, I believe that we are to go to the picture
gallery of a Mr. Weednaar, with a friend who has
secured cards for us. I'm not invited to the luncheon,
but I'm keen to see the pictures."

"Very well," I said; "let me make plans for you;
I tell you what we'll do. I'll make it a holiday; I will
get my motor in from the country, and go around
with you and show you the sights. You want to
see 'Georgian' Philadelphia you say — we call it
'Colonial'; I know it well. I'll be your guide; you
shall take your photographs and make your sketches,
and in the afternoon we, too, will go out and see Mr.
Widener's pictures,— his name, by the way, is
Widener, not Weednaar,— and if I can find Harry

Widener, a scion of that house and a friend of mine, I'll get him to ask us out for lunch, and we will be there to welcome Bennett and his friend with their cards on their arrival. What, by the way, is the name of your friend to whom you owe your introduction to Mr. Widener?"

"A Mr. Hellman of New York; a bookseller, I believe; perhaps you know him, too."

"Perfectly," I said; "I probably owe him money at this very minute."

With this understanding and much pleased with each other, we parted for the night.

The next morning, at half-past nine, we met in the lobby, and I was presented to Arnold Bennett. At that time I do not remember that I had ever seen a photograph of him, and I was quite disillusioned by seeing a person quite lacking in distinction, in ill-fitting clothes, with two very prominent upper teeth which would have been invaluable had he taken to whistling, professionally.

"And you are the man," he said, "who has so captivated my friend Craig? He told me all about your escapade last night, over the breakfast-table, and in the excitement of narration he ate my eggs."

"No matter," said I; "you are going to lunch with the literati of the city — you ought not to worry over the loss of your eggs. But what is quite as important, who is giving the luncheon?"

"George Horace Lorimer," he replied.

"Then," said I, "you certainly need not worry over the loss of a pair of eggs. In an hour or two you'll be

GLORIA DEI (OLD SWEDES') CHURCH, PHILADELPHIA

glad you did not eat them, for Lorimer understands ordering a luncheon—no man better. I'm sorry for Craig, for he's lunching with me; but we shall join you during the afternoon at Mr. Widener's."

This seemed to upset Bennett completely. "But we are going to Mr. Weednaar's by appointment — we have cards —"

"I know, from George Hellman," I interrupted. "I don't need any cards. If Harry Widener is at home, we will lunch with him; if not, we will join you some time during the afternoon."

Bennett looked at me with astonishment. He had doubtless been warned of bunko-steerers, card-sharks, and confidence men generally. I appeared to him a very finished specimen, probably all the more dangerous on that account. We left him bewildered. He evidently thought that his friend would be the victim of some very real experiences before he saw him again. As we parted, he looked as if he wanted to say to Craig, "If you play poker with that man, you are lost"; but he didn't.

We Philadelphians do not boast of the climate of our city. During the summer months we usually tie with some town in Texas — Waco, I believe — for the honor of being the hottest place in the country; but in November it is delightful, and we have the finest suburbs in the world. If it were not for its out-lying districts, Philadelphia would be intolerable. But the day was fine, we were in high spirits, like boys out for a lark, which indeed we were, and I determined that our sightseeing should begin at the "Old Swedes Church,"— or, to give it its proper name, "Gloria Dei,"— and work our way from the southern part of the city to the northern, stopping at such old landmarks as would seem to afford material for Craig's pencil.

What a wonderful day it was; agreeable at the time and in retrospect delightful, if somewhat tinged with melancholy; for I chanced to read in an English newspaper not long ago of the death of my friend Craig, in some way a victim of the war. But looking back upon that day, everything seemed as joyous as the two quaintly carved and colored angels' heads, a bit of old Swedish decoration, which peered down upon us from the organ-loft of the old church, about which Craig went into ecstasies of delight; as well he might, for it is a quaint little box of a church, almost lost in the shipping and commerce that surrounds it. Built by the Swedes before the coming of William Penn, it stands on the bank of the Delaware, on the site of a block-house in which religious services had been held more than half a century before its erection.

Too few Philadelphians know this tiny toy church or attend its services: it is out of the beaten track of the tourist. But some of us, not entirely forgetful of old Philadelphia, love to visit it occasionally; and if the sermon gets wearisome, as sermons sometimes do, we can creep out stealthily and spend a few minutes prowling around the graveyard, in which interments are still made occasionally, looking at the tombstones, on which are curiously cut the now

ST. PETER'S CHURCH, PHILADELPHIA

almost illegible names of devout men and women who departed this life in faith and fear almost two centuries ago.

"But come now," I at last had to say, "this is our first, but by no means our best, church; wait until you see St. Peter's."

The ride from Old Swedes Church to St. Peter's has nothing to recommend it; but it is short, and we were soon standing in one of the finest bits of Colonial church architecture in America.

"Why," exclaimed Craig, "we have nothing more beautiful in London, and there is certainly nothing in New York or Boston that can touch it."

"Certainly, there is n't," I said; "and if you were a Philadelphian and had an ancestor buried in this church or within its shadow, you would not have to have brains, money, morals, or anything else. Of course, these accessories would do you no harm, and in a way might be useful; but the lack of them would not be ruinous, as it would be with ordinary folk." Then I spoke glibly the names of the dead whom, had they been living, I should scarce have dared to mention, so interwoven are they in the fabric of the social, or, as some might say, the unsocial life of Philadelphia.

"And these people," said Craig, "do they look like other people? do you know them?"

It was a delicate question. It was not for me to tell him that a collateral ancestor was a founder of the Philadelphia Assembly, or to boast of a bowing acquaintance with that charming woman, Mrs. John Markoe, whose family pew we were then reverently approaching. Craig could, of course, know nothing of what a blessed thing it is to be a member, not of St. Peter's, but of "St. Peter's set," which is a very different matter. But he fully appreciated the architectural charm of the building; and as we strolled about, he observed with the keenest interest the curious arrangement of the organ and altar at one end of the church, and the glorious old pulpit and reading-desk at the other, with a quite unnecessary sounding-board — for the church is not large — surmounting them like a benediction.

"How dignified and exclusive the square pews are," said Craig, "looking for all the world like the lord of the manor's, at home."

"Yes," said I, "and not half so exclusive as the people who occupy them. You could have made a very pretty picture of this church crowded with wealth and fashion and beauty a hundred and fifty years ago, if you had been lucky enough to have been born when there was color in the world; now we all look alike."

"I know," said Craig. "It's too bad."

I could have told him a good deal of the history of Christ Church, which we next visited. It is only a short distance from St. Peter's, indeed, in the early days Christ Church and St. Peter's formed one parish. The present structure was built in 1727, of bricks brought over from England. Architecturally, it is the finest church in Philadelphia, and so expensive it was for the congregation of two hundred years ago that, in order to finish its steeple and provide it with its

CHRIST CHURCH, PHILADELPHIA

fine chime of bells, recourse was had to a lottery! Indeed, two lotteries were held before the work was completed. Philadelphians all felt that they had a stake in the enterprise, and for a long time the bells were rung on every possible occasion. Queen Anne sent over a solid silver communion service, which is still in use; and the rector, Dr. William White, after the Revolution became the second bishop of the Episcopal Church in the United States of America, having finally been consecrated at Lambeth after years of discussion as to how the Episcopacy was to be carried on. So "Old Christ," as it is affectionately called, may properly be regarded as the Mother Church in this country. When Philadelphia was the capital of the nation, Washington attended it, as did John Adams, and Benjamin Franklin, occasionally — perhaps not often enough.

But our time was limited and there was much to see: Carpenter's Hall, and the State House with its beautiful windows, which Craig called Palladian, and its splendid Colonial staircase, from which I was quite powerless to draw his attention to the far-famed liberty bell.

"I know all about that," said Craig; "I've been reading it up; but if you can tell me in what single respect an Englishman has n't just as much liberty as an American, I shall be glad to listen."

I changed the subject; one always hates to discuss liberty with an Englishman, they have so many more "rights" than we have.

Having forgotten to point out the grave of our

greatest citizen, Benjamin Franklin, who, we love to tell Bostonians, was born in Philadelphia at seventeen years of age, we retraced our steps — if one can be said to retrace one's steps in a motor — to the Christ Church burying-ground at Fifth and Arch streets. There, peering through the iron railing, we read the simple inscription carved according to his wish on the flat tomb: "Benjamin and Deborah Franklin, 1790." I have always regretted that I did not avail myself of the opportunity once offered me of buying the manuscript, in Franklin's hand, of the famous epitaph which he composed in a rather flippant moment, in 1728, for his tombstone. The original is, I believe, among the Franklin papers in the State Department at Washington, but he made at least one copy, and possibly several. The one I saw reads:—

THE BODY

of

BENJAMIN FRANKLIN

PRINTER

(Like the cover of an old book
Its contents torn out
And stript of its lettering and gilding)
Lies here, food for worms.
But the work shall not be lost
For it will (as he believed) appear once more
In a new and more elegant edition

Revised and corrected
by
THE AUTHOR

No doubt the plain marble slab, with the simple name and date (for Franklin needs no epitaph in Philadelphia), is more dignified, but I have always wished that his first idea had been carried out.

As we were only a stone's throw from the Quaker Meeting-House, we paid it a hasty visit, and I confessed, in reply to a question, that, often as I had passed the austere old brick building, I had never entered it before, although I had always intended to.

At last I looked at my watch — unnecessarily, for something told me it was lunch-time. We had had a busy morning. Craig had made sketches with incredible rapidity, while I bought photographs and picture-postals by the score. We had not been idle for a moment, but there was more to be seen: Fairmount,— not the Park, there was no time for that, and all parks are more or less alike although ours is most beautiful,— but the old-time "water-works," beautifully situated on the hillside, terraced and turreted, with its three Greek temples, so faultlessly proportioned and placed as to form what Joe Pennell says is one of the loveliest spots in America and which, he characteristically adds, we in Philadelphia do not appreciate. But Craig did. It was a glorious day in mid-November; the trees were in their full autumn regalia of red and gold; the Schuylkill glistened like silver in the sun, and in the distance tumbled, with a gentle murmur of protest at being disturbed, over its dam into the lower level, where it becomes a river of use if not of beauty.

I thought how seldom do we business men pause

in the middle of the day to look at anything so free
from complications as a "view." My factory was
within ten minutes' walk; there, penned up amidst
dirt and noise, I spend most of my waking hours,
discussing ways and means by which I may increase
the distance between myself and the sheriff, and
neglecting the beauty which unfolds itself at my very
door. I determined in future to open my eyes occasionally; but hunger put an end to my meditations.
Food is required even on the most perfect day; by
this time the literati must have met — and parted.
Back to the city we sped, lunched at my club, thence
to "Lynnewood Hall," the palatial residence of Mr.
Widener, some miles from the centre of the city.

On our arrival we were ushered, through the main
entrance-hall, beautifully banked with rare flowers,
into the gallery in which is housed one of the finest collections of pictures in America. Bennett and George
Hellman were already there, and Mr. Widener, the
old gentleman who had formed the collection, was
doing the honors. Harry, his grandson, was there, too,
and, to the amazement of Bennett, welcomed me
with outstretched arms. "I got your telephone message, but too late to connect with you; I've been in
New York. Why did you not come to lunch? You
were not at your office. I left messages for you everywhere."

Bennett looked greatly relieved: so I was not an
intruder after all, and, wonderful to relate, nothing
had happened to Craig.

Mr. Widener seemed relieved to see me, and I soon

THE OLD "WATER WORKS" IN FAIRMOUNT PARK, PHILADELPHIA

understood the reason. He did not know who his guest was. "Who is this man?" he whispered to me.

"Arnold Bennett, the distinguished English author," I replied.

"Does he know anything about pictures?" he asked.

"I have no doubt he does," I replied. "Here is a man who certainly does."

I presented Craig who, to the great relief of his host, was vocal. And then I saw how things had been going. Bennett, with his almost uncanny power of observation, had seen and doubtless understood and appreciated everything in the gallery, but had remained mute; an "Oh!" or an "Ah!" had been all that Mr. Widener had been able to extract from him. The old gentleman had seemingly been playing to an empty house, and it irked him. Craig had the gift of expression; knew that he was looking at some of the masterpieces of the world, and said so.

We strolled from one gallery to another, and then it was suggested that perhaps we would care to see — But the afternoon was going; the party had to be in New York at a certain hour; it was time to move on.

"Spend another night in Philadelphia," I said to Craig; "you must not go without seeing Harry's books. After a while, there will be tea and toast and marmalade and Scotch and soda; life will never be any better than it is at this minute."

Craig did not require much urging. Why should he? We were honored guests in one of the finest houses in the country, in a museum, in fact, filled to

overflowing with everything that taste could suggest
and money buy; and for host we had the eldest son of
the eldest son of the house, a young man distinguished
for his knowledge, modesty, and courtesy. We went
to Harry's apartment, where his books were kept, and
where I was most of all at home. Finally his mother
joined us. In the easy give-and-take of conversation
time passed rapidly, and finally it was time to go, and
we said good-bye. It was my last visit to "Lynnewood Hall" as Harry's guest. Five months later,
almost to a day, he found his watery grave in the
Atlantic, a victim of the sinking of the Titanic.

On our way back to our hotel, we agreed that we
would go to the theatre and have supper afterward;
there was just time to change, once again gnawing a
sandwich. By great good fortune there was a real
comedy playing at one of the theatres; seats were
secured without unusual difficulty, and we were soon
quietly awaiting the rise of the curtain. After the
performance we had supper, which had been ordered
in advance. We were at the end of a perfect day, a
red-letter day, a day never to be forgotten, Craig
said. We had known each other something like
twenty-four hours, yet we seemed like old friends.

"I can't hope to give you such a day as we have
had, when you come to London, but you'll look me
up, won't you?"

"Yes, of course, and meanwhile I want you to do
something for me."

"Anything, my dear boy; what is it?"

"I want a presentation copy of 'Buried Alive' with

OLD BRIDGE OVER THE THAMES AT SONNING
From a water-color by Frank Craig

an inscription in it from Arnold Bennett, and on a fly-leaf I want a little pencil sketch by you."

"Righto, I'll send it directly I get to New York."

But I had to wait several days before I received a small package by express, which, on opening, I found to be a beautiful little water-color painting by Craig of the picturesque old stone bridge over the Thames at Sonning! and in another package, the book, "Buried Alive," with a characteristic inscription. The author was doubtful of my identity to the last, for he wrote: "To Mr. Newton of Philadelphia, I believe, with best wishes from Arnold Bennett."

XI

A SANE VIEW OF WILLIAM BLAKE

For a long time I hesitated over this title. It is very daring, and it may be misleading. Who shall say that I am sane and that William Blake was not? The fact that the policeman on the street-corner leaves me unmolested, and that the president of my bank receives me politely when I call upon him, proves nothing. I am not deceived by the fact that the pastor of my church — I have n't a church, and if I had, it would n't have a pastor — nods pleasantly when we meet. Nor is the statement of my friends, that I am mad, convincing — least of all, to me. Most of our friends are mad, but they are not dangerous. To say that a man is mad is merely a way we have of saying that his opinion does not coincide with ours, that is all. The question, Was Blake mad? has been too much stressed; it is not important; certainly he was not more mad than many who have written about him. Let us leave the question for later discussion; it may be that we shall not return to it; it may be that our paper, or your patience, will give out first.

Let me begin again. It is now almost, if not quite, thirty-five years ago that, in company with one of my oldest friends, the Reverend Lawrence B. Ridgley, I visited Walden Pond, and as was then the custom,—

Painted by T. Phillips R.A.

Engraved by L. Schiavonetti V.A.

William Blake

London, Published by R.H. Cromek, Newman S! May 1.st 1808.

WILLIAM BLAKE

From frontispiece to Blair's Grave

and may still be, for aught I know,— threw a stone upon the pile which marks the spot on which Thoreau built his hut, in which he lived for something over two years. The throwing of the stone was an act of reverence; in an instant it was not recognizable: it was just one more stone, not increasing perceptibly the size of the pile; but the fact that I had added a stone gave me pleasure, and this paper on William Blake may properly be regarded as another tiny stone erected to his honor. It can chiefly affect one person only, namely, the writer. I can neither add to nor detract from Blake's fame.

Nor have I any theory to propound in regard to the so-called prophetic or mystical books; I have read most of them with such care as I could, but they have made no lasting impression on my mind. I come to the surface gasping for breath, confused, bewildered, and convinced that any *literary* merit they may have is not worth the effort required in attempting to comprehend the thoughts,— if thoughts they are,— so involved, so contradictory, so curiously strung together, and dealing with the personification of emotions rather than with ideas. That these emotions masquerade under uncouth names, hard to pronounce and troublesome to remember, only adds to my difficulty, and having said this much, let me say that I, for one, would not have them different: their very obscurity only adds to their interest. As *works of art*, to which tags of some sort must be given, they are just what is indicated.

The mythology that Blake created was, so to speak,

the overflow, the waste product, of his mind, and may
be regarded as relatively unimportant. We should
look at the pages of "Urizen," "Thel," "Milton,"
"America," "Europe," and the rest, as the greatest
works of art produced in England and among the
greatest in the world, and let us not seek to know too
much. When we look at Rodin's statue, The Thinker,
we do not ask, "What was he thinking of?" we bend
the knee. In like manner, let us bow in reverence
before these great works of Blake's imagination. I
am not sympathetic with explanations which only
increase our bewilderment. To be told that every
gesture, every pose, has a meaning, detracts from my
enjoyment. I have tried to be sympathetic with the
views held by some of his admirers, but without success. If the right leg of Palamabron or Urizen is advanced, benign spirits are in the ascendant: if Rahab
raises her left arm, evil spirits have sway, you tell me.
Here we part company. It may be so; I do not know,
I do not care; with Browning, I would say, —

Did Shakespeare so, then the less Shakespeare he.

I am treading on delicate ground. Here, you see,
the personal equation comes in. I am not a student
or a mystic, but a twentieth-century man of affairs,
a manufacturer of electrical machinery, having problems of my own to solve which leave me little time to
deal with the anfractuosities — this was a favorite
word of my friend Dr. Johnson — of the minds of the
critics. For them the earth trembles and the sky is
overcast. I am not of their world; their atmosphere
I cannot breathe. I see lightning but no light, smoke

but no fire; I grasp nothing. Even Swinburne, possessed of a most far-fetched if not actually unsound judgment, admits that he cannot always understand; and to the destination at which Swinburne fails to arrive, I am reluctant to set out.

But it is time for me to begin. Dr. Johnson published his great dictionary in 1755. Two years later, near Golden Square in London, William Blake was born. There is no relation between the two events other than that they both took place in pretty nearly the dead centre of the eighteenth century.

Some would say that the words "dead centre" are particularly applicable to the period under discussion. Pope was dead. He died in 1744, and few would have had the temerity to inform Dr. Johnson that poetry was dead, too. In conversation with Boswell, he said, "Sir, a thousand years may elapse before there shall appear another poet like Pope." My friend Amy Lowell would doubtless exclaim, "Let us hope so!" But to Dr. Johnson, Pope and poetry were synonymous terms.

In these days of many small reputations and no single dominating figure, it is difficult for us to understand the immense vogue and following of a poet who could write such a couplet as

> Why has not man a microscopic eye?
> For this plain reason — man is not a fly.

But Pope, if he had little sweetness, certainly compacted wisdom in a most extraordinary manner.

> Know then thyself, presume not God to scan;
> The proper study of mankind is man.

Lines from Pope — or perhaps it would be more exact to say, couplets — intrude themselves on us unconsciously. Bartlett has page after page of quotations from Pope, and from Blake not a single one; and Pope's poetry, which so delighted Dr. Johnson that he said, "If Pope is not a poet, it is useless to look for one," is largely typical of the verse that distinguished the eighteenth century. I do not forget Gray, but it was reserved for a later period fully to appreciate the author of the "Elegy Wrote [1] in a Country Churchyard." If you think that I detain you unnecessarily with these details, it is because the background against which Blake appeared, and the nature of his surroundings, are most important for any appreciation of him.

Blake's father was a small but respectable tradesman — a Dissenter, probably a Swedenborgian. His son received little or no education and was early apprenticed to an engraver, one Basire, from whom he learned his trade. We hear of him making drawings of the statues and monuments in Westminster Abbey, and we know that he was influenced all his life by these studies and that he preferred to draw from the artistic abominations in the Abbey rather than from life; this explains much.

A perfectly proportioned male or female figure had little charm for Blake, if one can judge from those he drew. He could not see what we see, but, on the

---

[1] The word "Wrote" is indicative of the first edition, which is now worth five thousand dollars. When "wrote" became "written," as it did in the later editions, the value sinks to a few shillings.

SAMUEL, SAUL AND THE WITCH OF ENDOR
(1 Samuel xxviii, 12–21)

From original painting. No. 149 of the W. M. Rossetti Catalogue

other hand, we cannot see what he saw; and who of
us shall say that we can see as much as Blake? His
figures are, for the most part, out of drawing, exag-
gerated, usually elongated. If a man or woman
crouching on the ground should suddenly stand up,
he, or she, would stand seven feet tall. Yet he is not
a caricaturist, as my words might suggest; for somehow, somewhere, he learned to develop his mind, his
imagination, so that, if he ever remained eccentric as
a draughtsman and dry and hard as an engraver, he
became the greatest imaginative artist that England
ever produced.

England is supreme in poetry rather than in painting. The average Englishman, if he cares for painting
at all, outside of portraiture, wishes a picture that
tells a story; and the sillier the story, the better he
likes it. I chanced to see in the window of a shop not
long ago a picture that illustrates what I mean. A
simpering woman, without a stitch of clothes on, was
coming down a short flight of marble steps, holding
in front of her a bit of red-plush curtain. Is it Susanna
preparing to entice the elders? No. A horse in the
distance supplies the clue; and now we know that we
are playing Peeping Tom, and that Lady Godiva is
preparing to ride. The picture is characteristic of
English art at its very worst; as yet Blake has influenced it very little. But listen to an extract from
a letter which I received a few months ago from
Japan.

"A friend is asking me to send you a copy of my
book on William Blake. It is not a small pleasure for

me if I could add my humble book to your splendid collection of Blake's original works. The book, which appeared in 1914, however, has been all sold out and is out of print, and I can get it neither from the publisher nor from the bookshops, and it becomes almost impossible to obtain it even in the second-hand. Only one copy of it is left in my hands now. But the second enlarged edition, at which I am engaging now, will appear by the end of this year, so I decided to send the latter to you. Perhaps you will be surprised if you understand that Blake, who has been neglected so long by his countrymen, is now one of the most favorite artists in our young public here in Japan."

But this is a digression.

Blake, when he was twenty-five years old, married Catherine Boucher, a girl poorer than himself and of no education whatever. At the time of their marriage she was unable either to read or write. Enough has been said: they lived happily together, she merged her life in his, and his work constituted his life. Never was genius more industrious; whether in London, or in Lambeth, or in Felpham with his friend Hayley, never was he for a minute idle. It is one thing to write volume after volume; it is another thing to write, illustrate, engrave, print, illuminate, and himself sell a long series of volumes for which we should have to invent the phrase, "which must be seen to be appreciated," were it not already in use. It has been a great misfortune for Blake's fame, and a still greater misfortune for the world, that he must be studied in first editions. During his lifetime he was almost entirely neglected. After he died in 1827, he was for a time forgotten; so much so that Alexander Gilchrist, to whom we are chiefly indebted for what we know of him, called him "Pictor Ignotus."

Now first editions of Blake are excessively rare in these days; their prices run into, not hundreds, but thousands of dollars. They can be seen only here and there, in museums or in the private collections of rich men. That I have a few proves nothing — have I not been called mad? Well, about Blake, I am. There are, to be sure,

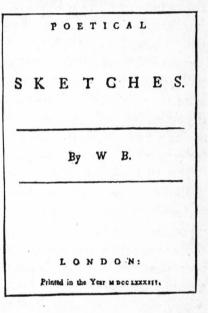

the reprints of that great student and enthusiast, William Muir, who about thirty-five years ago elected to bring out, through Bernard Quaritch, a number of exquisite facsimiles; but they were published in very limited editions,— only fifty copies,— they are now out of print and costly, and it is no exaggeration to say that such reproductions of Blake's pages in black and white as are available bear the same resemblance to the originals that a charcoal sketch does to an oil painting.

Blake's first literary work was his "Poetical Sketches," 1783 — a slender volume of the greatest poetical significance. It ushered in a kind of poetry unknown since the immediate followers of the Elizabethans; and if you think of Burns at this moment, as you may, I would remind you that the Kilmarnock edition, the first edition of Burns, appeared in 1786.

You have read how the fakirs in India put a little earth in a flower-pot, dropped in a few seeds, covered the flower-pot with a paper funnel, made a few prayers and incantations, removed the paper, and lo! a miracle had been performed — a rose tree in full bloom was revealed. Such a miracle was performed by William Blake. Out in the sordid streets of Soho he gathered a nosegay of lyrics such as had not blown in a century or more, and he called them "Poetical Sketches." This volume, printed but never published, is so rare that Gilchrist said of it : "After some years of vain attempt I am forced to abandon the idea of myself owning the book. There is, of course, none where at any rate there should be one — in the British Museum." This in 1863. I feel sure there is one there now; nevertheless, this little volume is of the utmost rarity.

In considering the poetical work of Blake, one must keep the background against which it appeared well in mind, and remember that the verse in this slender volume was written by a boy between his twelfth and twentieth years. I shall not detain you with the fragment of a drama in blank verse, remarkable as it is; but I must be allowed to give a few lines from

From plate engraved by William Blake

From original drawing by William Blake for Mary Wollstonecroft's "Original Stories"

several lyrics, than which there are none finer.   The
quantity is small, but the quality is supreme.

TO SPRING

O thou, with dewy locks, who lookest down
Thro' the clear windows of the morning; turn
Thine angel eyes upon our western isle,
Which in full choir hails thy approach, O Spring!

And reminding us of Herrick, of whom I am sure
Blake never heard, is his song, "My silks and fine
array," and "I love the jocund dance"; and then
his fourteen-line poem,— it is not a sonnet,— which
reads, in part: —

TO THE EVENING STAR

Thou fair-hair'd angel of the evening,
Now, whilst the sun rests on the mountains, light
Thy bright torch of love; thy radiant crown
Put on, and smile upon our evening bed!
Smile on our loves; and, while thou drawest the
Blue curtains of the sky, scatter thy silver dew
On every flower that shuts its sweet eyes
In timely sleep.   Let thy west wind sleep on
The lake; speak silence with thy glimmering eyes,
And wash the dusk with silver.

But you will not, I am sure, long wish to see a
middle-aged book-collector washing the dusk with
silver or, indeed, with anything else.   But how many
were there who, in 1783, took this for poetry?   The
non-success of this volume made it difficult, if not
impossible, for Blake to secure a publisher for his
next volume, and this fact influenced his entire life.

We now come to the "Songs of Innocence" (1789),
and to the "Songs of Experience" (1794), of some-

what lesser merit. In regard to these, I have a theory; namely, that Blake got his inspiration, or rather the idea of writing these lovely verses, from a paragraph in Dr. Watt's "Divine Songs." He must have known that remarkable book, of which its careful bibliographer, Wilbur Macey Stone, asserts that over five hundred editions have been printed in England and America. I was examining some time ago a presentation copy of the first edition of this excessively rare little book — it was published in 1715 and only two copies are known — in the Pierpont Morgan Library, under the watchful eye of Miss Thurston, who presides over the English books in this wonderful collection,— Miss Greene busying herself with some such matter as Coptic manuscripts the while!— when this paragraph met my eye. Referring to the slight character of the "Divine Songs," Dr. Watts said: "I wish some happy and condescending genius would undertake [to write] for the use of children and perform much better [than I have been able to do]." Here then, if I am not at fault, in such verses as "Let dogs delight to bark and bite," and "How doth the little busy bee," Blake found the raw material which his "happy and condescending genius" transmuted into such exquisite verses as "Little Lamb, who made thee?" and "Tiger, tiger, burning bright."

Be this as it may, Blake wrote his songs with so much genius that no publisher would touch them, and we owe the Blake that we know best to the fact that he decided to become his own publisher. Let me tell the story over again of how a vision came to

BLAKE'S CANTERBURY PILGRIMS

STOTHARD'S CANTERBURY PILGRIMS

him in the night, and revealed to him a method by
which he could produce his songs; and fittingly the
first song so produced was "The Piper."

> Piping down the valleys wild,
>   Piping songs of pleasant glee,
> On a cloud I saw a child,
>   And he laughing said to me : —
>
> "Pipe a song about a lamb."
>   So I piped with merry cheer.
> "Piper, pipe that song again."
>   So I piped; he wept to hear.
>
> "Drop thy pipe, thy happy pipe,
>   Sing thy songs of happy cheer."
> So I sung the same again,
>   While he wept with joy to hear.
>
> "Piper, sit thee down and write
>   In a book that all may read" —
> So he vanish'd from my sight;
>   And I pluck'd a hollow reed,
>
> And I made a rural pen,
>   And I stain'd the water clear,
> And I wrote my happy songs
>   Every child may joy to hear.

The story is told by Gilchrist that, sending Mrs.
Blake out with half-a-crown, all he had in the world,
he expended 1s. and 10d. for the simple materials
necessary for putting into practice the revelation.

"Upon that investment of 1s. and 10d., he started
what was to prove a principal means of support
through his future life — the series of poems and
writings illustrated by coloured plates, often highly

finished afterwards by hand, which became the most efficient and durable means of revealing his genius to the world. This method, to which he henceforth consistently adhered, of multiplying his works, was quite an original one. It consisted in a species of engraving in relief both words and designs. The verse was written and the designs and marginal embellishments outlined on the copper with an impervious liquid, probably the ordinary stopping-out varnish of engravers. Then all . . . the remainder of the plate was eaten away with acid, so that the outline of letter and design was left prominent, as in stereotype. From these plates he printed off in any tint, yellow, brown, blue, required to be the . . . ground colour in his fac-similes; red he used for the letterpress. The page was then coloured up by hand in imitation of the original drawing, with more or less variety of detail in the local hues."

May I give another song — still of innocence?

THE LAMB

Little lamb, who made thee?
Dost thou know who made thee,
Gave thee life and bid thee feed
By the stream and o'er the mead;
Gave thee clothing of delight,
Softest clothing, woolly, bright;
Gave thee such a tender voice
Making all the vales rejoice?
   Little lamb, who made thee?
   Dost thou know who made thee?

Little lamb, I'll tell thee,
Little lamb, I'll tell thee.

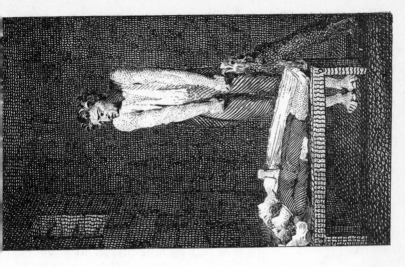

From plate engraved by William Blake

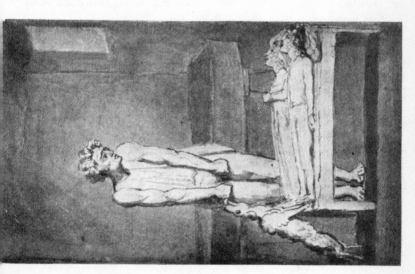

From original drawing by William Blake for Mary
Wollstonecraft's "Original Stories"

He is called by thy name,
For He calls himself a Lamb.
He is meek and He is mild,
He became a little child.
I a child and thou a lamb,
We are called by His name.
     Little lamb, God bless thee,
     Little lamb, God bless thee.

And one more, from "Experience," which Lamb called
glorious, as indeed it is.

THE TIGER

Tiger, tiger, burning bright,
In the forests of the night,
What immortal hand or eye
Could frame thy fearful symmetry?

In what distant deeps or skies
Burnt the fire of thine eyes?
On what wings dare he aspire?
What the hand dare seize the fire?

And what shoulder, and what art,
Could twist the sinews of thy heart?
And when thy heart began to beat,
What dread hand and what dread feet?

What the hammer? what the chain?
In what furnace was thy brain?
What the anvil? what dread grasp
Dare its deadly terrors clasp?

When the stars threw down their spears,
And water'd heaven with their tears,
Did he smile his work to see?
Did He who made the lamb make thee?

Tiger, tiger, burning bright
In the forests of the night,

What immortal hand or eye
Dare frame thy fearful symmetry?

There are to-day no two opinions as to these poems : they are exquisite ; and with these "Songs," Blake had, in my judgment, delivered his message.   What he wrote afterward,— if we except the lovely poem on England, which I forbear to quote, in the "Milton" (1804),— although in bulk ten times greater than what had gone before, has little value.   Published in the same manner as the "Songs," and growing more elaborate as Blake came to feel more at home with the medium he had chosen, his prophetic or mystical books are supreme as works of art.   Of some of them very few copies are known, and no two copies are alike, for the reason that, after an impression had been pulled from the copper plate in some color, like dull red or brown, they were worked over by hand, tints and backgrounds were added.   In some cases, where Blake had secured a generous or opulent customer, gold and brilliant colors were used so freely that the text is greatly obscured, and one almost forgets that the lovely work of art before him was intended to be read as a printed page as well as studied as a picture.   For this reason his books are difficult to describe or to evaluate.   Another difficulty is that they are scattered broadcast over the world, and a man writing on Blake in London would be crippled without the knowledge that would be afforded by consulting the great private collections of this country ; in like manner, a man writing here would be helpless unless he had studied the treasures in the

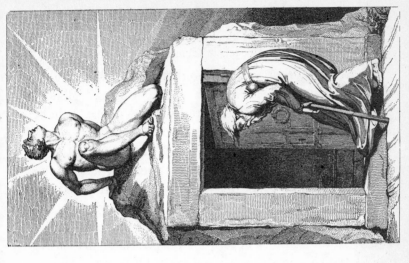

*From engraved plate in Blair's "Grave," after Blake's design,
by Louis Schiavonetti*

*From large preliminary sketch of Death's Door
by William Blake*

British Museum, the Tait Gallery, and such private collections as Captain Stirling's and Mr. Graham Robertson's.

Collectors are awaiting with the keenest interest the publication of a Blake bibliography, which, it is an open secret, is being prepared by my friend Mr. Geoffrey Keynes, of London, for the Grolier Club. It will no doubt settle many controversial points — and as certainly raise many others which supposedly had been settled years ago.

Blake's prophetic books so-called, can be read, I contend, only as task-work, or by the enthusiast seeking, as the old colored preacher said, to unscrew the unscrewable. To them largely is due the prevalent belief that Blake was unsound in mind, if not actually mad. Throughout them, and here and there in his writings, are curious little couplets or jingles, epigrams and the like, which might have come from the pen of Benjamin Franklin — of all men in the world!

> I was angry with my friend,
> I told my wrath, my wrath did end.
> I was angry with my foe,
> I told it not, my wrath did grow.

Or

> A truth that's told with bad intent
> Beats all the lies you can invent.

Or the line that Margot has placed on the title-page of her autobiography: "Prudence is a rich ugly old maid wooed by incapacity." In "The Marriage of Heaven and Hell," Blake has several pages of these curious proverbs.

My own interest in Blake dates from 1893, during which year Herbert Gilchrist, the son of the man to whom all Blake lovers are so greatly indebted, came to Philadelphia and exhibited at our Academy of the Fine Arts a large and thoroughly bad picture of Cleopatra. Not to digress needlessly, I saw a good deal of him, and purchased from him several small Blake sketches, notably one which William Michael Rossetti refers to in his "Descriptive Catalogue," Death and Hell teem with Life; and about that time I got into correspondence with William Linnell, the son of the man who did so much to keep Blake's body and soul together during the last years of his life, relative to a set of proofs I had purchased of Blake's last, and by many regarded as his greatest, work, his illustrations of the Book of Job. At the Buxton Forman sale in New York several winters ago, I was fortunate enough to secure the ten original India-ink sketches, six of which appeared in the first edition of Mary Wollstonecraft's "Original Stories From Real Life, with Conversations calculated to Regulate the Affections and Form the Mind to Truth and Goodness" — as the title goes. The frontispiece is characteristically Blakian, and is a good example of the curiously elongated figure of which Blake was so fond. As these plates were engraved as well as designed by him, it will be interesting to give several reproductions side by side.

What difference does it make that these drawings, like so much of Blake's work, are out of focus. It would have been an easy thing for the artist to

WHEN THE MORNING STARS SANG TOGETHER

From a photograph taken from the original drawing for this publication.   Never before photographed

represent the human body with reasonable perfection, but he was more interested in the idea that his work suggests than in technical accuracy. In other words, he drew for the mind rather than for the eye.

In the course of years I came to have most of the impor- tant books about Blake, and gradually the less important and expensive books for which he designed or engraved the illus- trations. Finally, a fine copy of the "Songs" came my way, followed by a "Marriage of Heaven and Hell." Just about this time Mr. Huntington became interested and I side- stepped, quickly; for when Mr. Hunting- ton takes up a sub- ject, it is a case of "all hope abandon."

ORIGINAL STORIES

FROM

REAL LIFE;

WITH

CONVERSATIONS,

CALCULATED TO

REGULATE THE AFFECTIONS,

AND

FORM THE MIND

TO

TRUTH AND GOODNESS.

BY MARY WOLLSTONECRAFT.

LONDON:

PRINTED FOR J. JOHNSON, NO. 72, ST. PAUL'S CHURCH-YARD.

1791.

When his appetite was momentarily appeased, I ventured into the open again; and about that time Mr. Herschel V. Jones's books came on the market. I felt that I was going to succumb to temptation; I tried to steady myself, but came down with a crash. I think Mitchell Kennerley was to some extent responsible for my fall, because in his private office he called my particular attention to the "Gates of Paradise," talked

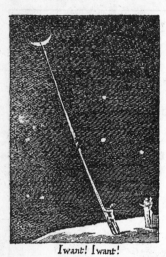

I want! I want!

THE MOON

From a tiny and very rare plate by William Blake. From the "Gates of Paradise."

learnedly about the "Keys to the Gates," in Mr. White's possession, showed me the "America," "Europe," and "Thel," and, in brief, stimulated me beyond endurance. I feared John L. Clawson of Buffalo, feared and hated him; but he was momentarily engaged with Restoration dramatists, and that's a subject well calculated to keep one's mind occupied and one's purse empty, as even he knows. Finally the day of the sale came: luck was with me, and when the smoke of battle cleared away, I had as nice a little cluster of Blakes as any man may hope to see. But my bank account was a ruin.

On the wall just opposite my desk hangs a fine copy of Blake's Canterbury Pilgrims. No finer story was ever told than that of the Pilgrims setting out from the Tabard Inn for the shrine of Thomas à Becket at Canterbury. It is an epitome of the life of the time, and Stothard's painting was exhibited far and near, and was deservedly popular, whereas

ONE OF THE FAMOUS PLATES IN BLAKE'S BOOK OF JOB

Printed for comparison with the reproduction from the original drawing

poor Blake, whose idea it originally was, found his picture scoffed at.[1] Few persons came to his little exhibition and bought for half a crown (which also included admission) his "Descriptive Catalogue"; still fewer paid the four-guinea subscription for the engraved plate. The failure of the enterprise would have broken the artist's heart, had his heart been of the breaking kind.

Notwithstanding its faulty technique, the engraving makes a strong intellectual appeal. It has a mediæval look, in keeping with the subject; and Lamb, with unerring taste, preferred it to the more popular picture by Stothard. Time works wonders in mat-

[1] My copy was a Christmas present from my wife several years ago. It came about in this way. My Blake enthusiasm was by this time no longer a secret. It was Christmas eve; my wife, faithful soul, had been decorating a Christmas tree in one of our city squares for the fatherless children of France. It had been, and was, raining; she was wet, cold, disheveled, and discouraged. Suddenly it occurred to her: "Why, I've bought no presents for the family; we shall have no Christmas at home — no wreaths, no tree, nothing." It was growing dark; there was no time to lose. In a few moments, with armlets of Christmas wreaths, some parcels, and a dripping umbrella, she presented herself at the door of the Rosenbach Galleries in Walnut Street, and inquired for my friend, the doctor. "I think he's busy," wisely observed the boy at the door, not liking the appearance of the customer, and reaching out his hand for her umbrella. "No doubt he is," was her reply, "but he will see me for a moment. — Doctor, I want a present for Mr. Newton, something handsome, something he wants." — "I have the very thing," said Rosy. (Of course he had, he always has.) "This," he continued, "is just what he wants for his Blake collection: it's a magnificent proof on India paper of The Canterbury Pilgrims; it's expensive, but very rare." — "I don't care about the price, for I shall hand the bill to him when it comes in." (This to Rosy of all men; the most astute bandit out of Wall Street!) And that's how this rare engraving comes to hang right alongside Stothard's print on the same subject, which came from the Halsey collection.

ters of art, as in other things. Stothard is by way of being forgotten, while Blake has at last come into his own.

By 1808 Blake was practically through with his prophetic books, and was busying himself making sketches illustrating Blair's "Grave." It was his intention to cut the plates himself, but in some way the original designs passed into the possession of one Cromek, an art publisher, who thought that the artist was sufficiently recompensed by the payment of a guinea and a half each for these magnificent drawings. Cromek employed the graceful and popular engraver, Schiavonetti, to engrave the plates, and the publication was very successful; but poor Blake, defrauded of his work, made nothing by its success. He has pilloried the publisher for all time in the couplet: —

> A petty, sneaking knave I knew:
> Oh, Mr. Cromek! how do you do?

Another work, of less merit, but of value as evidence of Blake's immense industry and originality, is the series of designs for Young's "Night Thoughts." The original drawings are in the possession of my friend Mr. W. A. White of New York. They number 537, and were completed, with much other work, in two years! What imagination! What industry!

We now come to his Illustrations of the Book of Job, which is perhaps the best known of all his works. These "inventions," as he called them, were engraved on copper by the artist himself, somewhat smaller in size than the original drawings, which are

THE BEGGAR'S OPERA.

After a painting by Hogarth, engraved by Blake; size of engraving 16¾ by 21 inches

in the most delicate and exquisite water-color. There
are two sets of these drawings; how many people
have seen either of them? As the Grolier Club Catalogue of the Blake Exhibition of 1905, in speaking
of the set first made, says, "There is something
pathetic in the picture of this solitary, unappreciated
old man (he was now well on to seventy years of age)
at work upon the noble story of Job and his sufferings." Both sets of drawings are now in this country: the original set finally passed from the Earl of
Crewe's collection into Mr. Morgan's library, and
the replicas are at this moment in the hands of
Gabriel Wells, the dealer, where they await, for only
a small fraction of their value, a discriminating pur-
chaser. Perhaps no art object now on sale in New
York is so well worth buying. Why it has not passed
into the possession of the Metropolitan Museum, or
some other, is a mystery. It would be a rare privilege to examine the two sets side by side. Both, so
Gilchrist says, are finely drawn and pure in color;
necessarily very much finer than the engravings of
the same subjects. Much was lost in translation to
copper. "If, therefore," as Gilchrist says, "the engravings are the best that Blake ever did, the drawings would seem by inference to be his greatest work."

Now think of it! Here is one of the great art
works of the world, which can be seen only by those
who are privileged to enter Mr. Morgan's library in
New York, or who attend from time to time the
public exhibitions of Blake's work. The tragedy
is that they are executed on so small a scale that an

ordinary letter-sheet would cover the whole design;
and so delicately and exquisitely colored are they,
that they cannot frequently be exposed to the light.
The series consists of 21 numbered plates; one of
them, "When the morning stars sang together," is
considered to be the finest thing Blake ever did.

I am not greatly impressed with Blake as an engraver, even in his universally admired Job plates;
his work is mannered, hard, and dry; he did not, I
think, love copper as an engraver should; the work
progressed too slowly, his hand only being employed,
his imagination shriveled, and he was unhappy.
Neither in Job nor in the Canterbury Pilgrims is
Blake's best engraving to be seen, but rather, as it
seems to me, in his designs to illustrate Hayley's
"Ballads," and in his fine large plate after Hogarth's
painting of the "Beggar's Opera."

Of the relative merits of the drawings, frequently
very elaborately colored, in his prophetic books, it is
difficult to speak; it depends so much upon the particular book that may be under the observation of the
critic.   Muir, who may be presumed to have seen
them all, says, "I consider the 'Songs of Innocence
and of Experience' the most beautiful book that has
ever been produced in England."   All things considered, I agree with him, although in my judgment
"Urizen" is the most powerful, the most Michel-
Angelesque of all the works of his imagination.   Mr.
White has a copy, unique, so far as is known, in this
country; and I am the proud owner of a full-page
original drawing for that book, reproduced as a

frontispiece to this publication. I own, too, the original sketches for the title-page to "America," as well as the book itself, which is very fine; but I think no drawing in it compares with the title-page of "Europe," which Blake himself regarded as one of his best designs. And so it goes.

We know into what verbal rhapsodies relatively unimportant examples of his work sometimes threw such writers as Gilchrist, Rossetti, Swinburne, and others, who attempted to translate Blake's indefinable art into words. What they failed in doing, I shall not attempt. And I have confessed that I cannot understand or follow his peculiar and personal mythology: I inspect his work whenever opportunity offers, praise it when I think I understand it, and keep silence when I do not. The creation of an imagination infinitely superior to that of Doré and comparable with that of Michael Angelo or Dante, whom alone he may be said to resemble, is more than enough for me; I do not expect fully to understand.

It is a great misfortune for the world that his canvas, his paper, his copper, was too small adequately to display the tremendous inventions of his genius. He who should have covered the dead walls of St. Paul's with frescoes was forced to content himself with bits of copper or scraps of paper smaller than this on which I write. It is hardly surprising that the greatest artist England ever produced should have been so completely neglected in his own lifetime.

Again I come back to Blake, the man. All his life he was misunderstood, ridiculed, insulted, and almost starved; yet listen to his words to a little girl shortly before he died: "May God make this world to you, my child, as beautiful as it h~~ been to me." Blake died in his seventieth year, and was buried in

DEATH'S DOOR.

From an early engraving by William Blake, full size.

Bunhill Fields Burying-Ground, that crowded Campo Santo in which were already interred two other great Nonconformists, Bunyan and Defoe. It is one of the ironies of fate that Blake, whose genius from his early youth to the day of his death was concerned with mortuary design, should lie in an unmarked and forgotten grave. In his work he repeated again and again an idea which was an especial favorite of his, that of an old man entering a tomb; he called it Death's Door. The germ of this exists in a pencil-sketch hardly larger than a postage-stamp, in the Rossetti manuscript, now the property of Mr. W. A. White. He used this design again and again, in "The Gates of Paradise," in "America," and finally in Blair's "Grave"; and I was fortunate enough to secure a large India-ink drawing of it about a year ago, when it came up for sale in London. Such a design, carved on stone, would have

MAGNIFICENTLY COLORED TITLE–PAGE TO "AMERICA," BY WILLIAM BLAKE

suitably marked his grave for all time; but it was not to be. Blake, ignored and neglected in his life, was destined to be forgotten for a time after his death; indeed, until Gilchrist, a full generation later, opened the Gates of Paradise and set free the soul of him who, unknown to his contemporaries, had put on immortality.

From one of Blake's last works.   Mr. Geoffrey Keynes thinks that it was intended for a bookplate

XII

MY OLD LADY, LONDON

I once heard a charming woman say at dinner, "I don't think I ever had quite as much fresh asparagus as I wanted." In like manner, I don't think I shall ever get as much of London as is necessary for my complete happiness. I love it early in the morning — before it rouses itself, when the streets are deserted; I love it when throngs of people — the best-natured and politest people in all the world — crowd its thoroughfares; and I love it, I think, best of all at sunset, when London in some of its aspects may be very beautiful. If I were a Londoner, I should never leave it, except perhaps for a day or two now and then, so that I could enjoy coming back to it.

The terrible world-upheaval through which we have just passed is responsible for my not having been in London for six years, and I greatly feared that those years might have left some unhappy imprint upon the Old Lady. She may, indeed, have lost a tooth or a wisp of hair; but aristocratic old ladies know how to conceal the ravages of time and circumstance, and as I looked around the railway station while my belongings were being stowed away in the "left-luggage" room, I saw only the usual crowd quietly going about its business; and then, as I stepped into my taxi and said, "Simpson's in the

Strand," and was being whirled over Waterloo Bridge, I said to myself, "Nothing has changed. Nothing has changed except that the fare, which was once eightpence, is now a shilling."

I said it again, with not quite the same certainty, when, after eating my piece of roast beef and a little mess of greens and a wonderful potato, I called the head waiter and complained that the meat was tough and stringy. "It is so," said that functionary; and he continued: "You see, sir, during the war we exhausted" (with careful emphasis upon the *h*) "our own English beef, and we are now forced to depend upon — " I looked him straight in the eye; he was going to say America, but changed his mind and said, "the Hargentine."

"Very neatly done," I said, ordering an extra half-pint of bitter and putting a sixpence in his hand; "to-morrow I'll have fish. I'm very sure that nothing can have happened to the turbot."

It was only a little after one when, leaving Simpson's, I lit a cigar and turned westward in quest of lodgings. As the Savoy was near at hand, I thought no harm would be done by asking the price of a large double-bedded room overlooking the river, with a bath, and was told that the price would be five guineas a day, but that no such accommodation was at that moment available. "I'm glad of it," I said, feeling that a temptation had been removed; for I have always wanted a room which looked out on the river.

I continued westward, inquiring at one hotel after

another, until, just as I was beginning to feel — not alarmed but — a trifle uneasy, I secured, not just what I wanted, but a room and a bath that would serve, at the Piccadilly.

I had been kept waiting quite a little time in the lobby, and as I looked about me there seemed to be a good many foreigners in evidence — a number of Spaniards and, I suspected, Germans. A fine manly young fellow with only one arm (how many such I was to see!), who manipulated the lift and to whom I confided my suspicions, replied, "Yes, sir; I believe they is, sir; but what are you going to do? They calls themselves Swiss!"

But in my anxiety to get to London I have forgotten to say a word about the Imperator, on which I crossed, or about the needless expense and delay to which one is subjected in New York, for no reason that I can see but that some of what Mr. Bryan called "deserving Democrats" may be fed at the public trough.

After being photographed and getting your passport and having it viséd by the consul of the country to which you are first going, and after assuring the officials of the Treasury Department that the final installment of your income tax will be paid, when due, by your bank,— though where the money is to come from, you don't in the least know,— you finally start for New York, to be there one day before the steamer sails, so that you may again present your passport at the Custom House for final inspection. I know no man wise enough to tell me what good purpose is

served by this last annoyance. With trunks and
suitcases, New York is an expensive place in which
to spend a night, and one is not in the humor for it:
one has started for Europe and has reached — New
York.

But, fearful that some hitch may occur, you wire
on for rooms and get them, and on "the day previous
to sailing," as the regulation demands, you present
yourself and your wife, each armed with a passport,
at the Custom House. Standing in a long line in a
corridor, you eventually approach a desk at which
sits a man consuming a big black cigar. Spreading
out your passport before him, he looks at it as if he
were examining one for the first time; finally with a
blue pencil he puts a mark on it and says, "Take it
to that gentleman over there," pointing across the
room. You do so; and another man examines it,
surprised, it may be, to see that it so closely resembles one that he has just marked with a red pencil.
He is just about to make another hieroglyph on the
passport, when he observes that the background of
your photograph is dark, and the regulations call for
light. He suspends the operation; is it possible that
you will be detained at the last moment? No! with
the remark "Get a light one next time," he makes a
little mark in red and scornfully directs you to
another desk. Here sits another man — these are
all able-bodied and presumably well-paid politicians
— with a large rubber stamp; it descends, and you
are free to go on board your ship — to-morrow.

The Imperator made, I think, only one trip in the

service of the company that built her; during the war she remained tied up to her pier in Hoboken; and when she was finally put into passenger service, she was taken over, pending final allocation, by the Cunard Line. She is a wonderful ship, with the exception of the Leviathan the largest boat afloat, magnificent and convenient in every detail, and as steady as a church. The doctor who examines my heart occasionally, looking for trouble, would have had a busy time on her; I fancy I can see him, drawing his stethoscope from his pocket and suspending it in his ears, poking round, listening in vain for the pulsation of her engines; no doubt fearful that he was going to lose his patient, he would have prescribed certain drops in water at regular intervals, and, finally, he would have sent her in a very large bill.

I am quite sure that I owe my comparatively good health to having been very abstemious in the matter of exercise. But it was my habit to take a constitutional each day before breakfast; this duty done, I was able to read and smoke thereafter with a clear conscience. Four and a half times around the promenade deck was a mile, the steward told me, and I can quite believe it. To relieve the monotony of this long and lonely tramp, I tried to learn by heart a letter which came to me just as we were sailing, in the form of a merry jingle, written by a master, or, should I say, a mistress of laughing rhyme, who loves to make fun of her friends. I never quite succeeded, but it reads this way : —

A HANSOM CAB; SOON TO BE SEEN ONLY IN THE LONDON MUSEUM

From a water-color in the possession of the author

Somewhere in Connecticut.
Somewhere in *September*, 1920.

A. Edward Newton : Dear Friend and Philosopher :
Also your wife (tho' you'll never be boss of her!)
So you're to sail on the good Imperator
O'er Byron's justly famed deep, dark blue water.
As I sat musing,— up here in Connecticut,—
Your letter reached me, and you can just bet I cut
Down to the shops of this hamlet Berkshirian,
Seeking a draught from the old spring Pierian.
For, I opined, no flowers or confections —
Only a *book* — for the Man of Collections.
Certain conventions admit of no lenities,
Only a *book* for the Man of "Amenities."
Down to the village I went with celerity,
Said to the Shopman with eager asperity,
"I want a book for one A. Edward Newton —
Something high-priced and a bit hifalutin.
For it's a parting gift — sort of a souvenir ;
No modern novel, dolled up in a new veneer!
Rather some old tome all leathery and lacquery,—
Some First Edition of Dickens or Thackeray —
Something that's truly a worth-while memorial
To one the *Atlantic* in lines editorial,
Says is 'of Letters a Doctor and Ornament'!"
(And I admit you're a handsome adornment!)
"Give me," I begged, "some unique *Enchiridion*,
Some precious copy of 'Epipsychidion,'
Some ancient Horn Book, or rare *Incunabula*,"—
Right here, his jaw dropped,— his eyes became globular ;
"Show me," I went on, "a binding *Zaehnsdorfian*,
To please this Minotaur Anthropomorphian ;
A tall Shakespeare quarto, an Omar Khayyám,
An early edition of Bacon or Lamb — "
"Oh, say," his eyes shone, "there's a butcher next door —
A quarter of Lamb you can get at *his* store!"
More in sorrow than anger, I murmured, "Good day."
Bookless, helpless, and hopeless, went sadly away.

And that is the reason, O A. Edward Newton,
No rare Rabelais, Rasselas or Rasputin
To you as a parting remembrance I send.
From my over-full heart I can merely commend
Your soul to your Maker, your luggage to Cook,
And waft you "Bon Voyage" in place of a *book*.
May your buys over there be far more than your sells,
Is the wish of yours faithfully,

CAROLYN WELLS.

Coming back to earth, or rather sea, after this
flight into the empyrean, I am bound to admit that
the Germans knew how to build and run ships. And
the beautiful part of the Imperator was that, though
you saw a German sign occasionally, not a German
word was heard. How completely, for the time being
at any rate, the German nation has been erased from
the sea! I sometimes doubt the taste of the English
singing "Rule, Britannia," it is so very true — now.

As we entered Southampton Water after a pleasant and quite uneventful voyage, we saw almost the
only sign of the war we were destined to see. A long
line, miles long, of what we should call torpedo-boat
destroyers, anchored in mid-stream, still wearing their
camouflage coloring, slowly rusting themselves away.
We landed on a clear warm September afternoon and,
Southampton possessing no charm whatever, we at
once took train for Winchester, which we reached in
time to attend service in the austere old cathedral.
The service was impressive and the singing better
than in most cathedrals, for the choir is largely recruited from the great school founded centuries ago
by William of Wykeham. After the service we stood

silently for a moment by the tomb of Jane Austen;
nor did we forget to lift reverently the carpet that
protects the tablet let into the tombstone of Isaak
Walton.   After tea, that pleasant function, we drove
out to the Hospital of St. Cross, beautiful and always
dear to me, being, as it is, the scene of Trollope's
lovely story, "The Warden."

Seated at home in my library, in imagination I love
to roam about this England, this "precious stone set
in the silver sea," which, now that the air has been
conquered, no longer serves it as a defensive moat;
but directly I find myself there, the lure of London
becomes irresistible, and almost before I know it I
am at some village railway station demanding my
"two single thirds" to Waterloo, or Victoria, or
wherever it may be.   So it was in this case.   I did,
however, take advantage of the delightful weather
to make a motor pilgrimage to Selborne, some fifteen
miles across country from Winchester.   A tiny copy
of White's "Natural History of Selborne" came into
my possession some forty years ago, by purchase, at
a cost of fifteen cents, at Leary's famous bookshop
in Philadelphia; and while I now display, somewhat
ostentatiously perhaps, Horace Walpole's own copy
of the first edition, I keep my little volume for reading and had it with me on the steamer.   "The
Wakes," the house in which Gilbert White was born
and in which he died, is still standing on what is by
courtesy called the main street of the little village,
which is, in its way, I suppose, as famous as any set-
tlement of its size anywhere.

The church of which he was rector, and in which he preached when he was not wandering about observing with unexampled fidelity the flora and fauna of his native parish, stands near the upper end of a tiny public square called the Plestor, or play place, which dates only from yesterday, that is to say, from 1271! Originally an immense oak tree stood in the centre, but it was uprooted in a great storm some two centuries ago and a sycamore now stands in its place. Encircling it is a bench on which the rude forefathers of the hamlet may sit and watch the children at play, and on which we should have sat but that we were more interested in the great yew which stands in the near-by churchyard. It is one of the most famous trees in England — a thousand years old they say, and looking old for its age; but it is so. symmetrical in its proportions that its immense size is not fully realized until one slowly paces round it and discovers that its trunk is almost thirty feet in circumference.

The church, which has luckily escaped the restorations so many parish churches have been compelled to undergo, is in no wise remarkable. Many Whites are buried therein; but our particular White, the one who has made Selborne notable among the villages of England, lies outside in the churchyard near the north wall of the chancel, the grave being marked by a half-sunken headstone on which one reads with difficulty two simple letters, "G. W." and a date, "26th June 1793"; but a tablet within the church records at greater length his virtues and distinctions.

There is nothing more exhausting than the elegance of a big hotel, and to move from a fashionable caravansary in Philadelphia to another in London or Paris is to subject one's self to the inconvenience of travel without enjoying any of its compensations. One wants to enjoy the difference of foreign countries rather than their somewhat artificial resemblances. At the end of a busy day, when one is tired, one wants peace, quiet, and simplicity — at least this one does; and so, when our attention was called to a small apartment in Albemarle Street, from the balcony of which I could throw a stone into the windows of Quaritch's bookshop. I closed the bargain instantly, and was soon by way of being a householder on a very small scale.

We had been told that "service" in England is a thing of the past, that it has disappeared with the war; but this was only one of the many discouraging statements which were to be entirely refuted in the experience. No one could have been better cared for than we, by a valet and maid, who brushed our clothes and brought us our breakfast; and shortly after ten each morning we started out upon our wanderings in whatever direction we would, alert for any adventure that the streets of London might afford. This is an inexpensive and harmless occupation, interesting in the event and delightful in retrospect. Is it Liszt who conjures us to store up recollections for consumption in old age? Well, I am doing so.

I know not which I enjoy most, beating the pavements of the well-known streets, which afford at every turn scenes that recall some well-known historic or literary incident, or journeying into some unexplored region, which opens up districts of hitherto unsuspected interest. Years ago, when slumming first

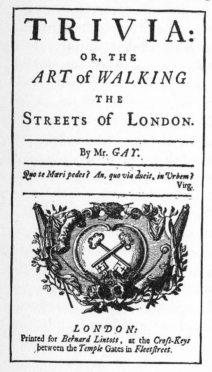

TRIVIA:

OR, THE

ART of *WALKING*

THE

STREETS of LONDON.

By Mr. *GAY*.

Quo te Mœri pedes? An, quo via ducit, in Urbem?
Virg.

LONDON:
Printed for *Bernard Lintott*, at the *Cross-Keys*
between the *Temple* Gates in *Fleetstreet.*

became fashionable, one never used to overlook Pettycoat Lane in far-off Whitechapel; of late years it has been cleaned up and made respectable —and uninteresting. But how many people are there who know that there is a very pretty slum right in the heart of things, only a short distance back of Liberty's famous shop in Regent Street? If interested in seeing how the other half lives, look it up when you are next in London, and you will be astonished at the way in which the pursuit of life, liberty, and happiness unfolds itself in a maze of little streets and courts all jumbled together. London has always been a city in which extremes meet: where wealth impinges upon poverty. Nowhere can greater contrasts be obtained than in that *terra incognita*, which lies just to the south

of Soho. The world lives, if not in the open, at least in
the streets, and food, fruit, fish, and furbelows are exposed for sale on barrows and trestles in what appears
to be unspeakable confusion. I had discovered this
curious slum years before my friend Lucas, that sympathetic wanderer in London, called attention to it in his
delightful volume, "Adventures and Enthusiasms."

But there is, to my mind, an even choicer little
backwater, just off Fleet Street — Nevill's Court,
which I first visited many years ago, during a memorable midnight ramble, in company with David
Wallerstein, a Philadelphia lawyer and an old friend,
who, by reason of his wide reading, retentive memory, and power of observation, seemed able to better
my knowledge of London even in a district where I
had thought myself peculiarly at home.

Nevill's Court runs east from Fetter Lane. One
enters it by an archway which may easily be passed
unnoticed, and to one's great surprise one comes suddenly upon a row of old mansions, one of which was
pointed out to me as once having been the town residence of the Earl of Warwick. "It was a grand 'ouse
in its day, sir," said a young woman in an interesting
condition, who was taking the air late one afternoon
when I first saw it, "but it's let out as lodgings now.
Keir Hardie, M.P., lodges here when he's in London;
he says he likes it here, it's so quiet."

"And how long have you lived here?" I inquired.

"Oh, sir, Hi 've always lived about 'ere in this court
or close to; Hi like living in courts, it's so quiet; it's
most like living in the country."

All the houses look out upon ample, if now sadly neglected, gardens, through the centre of which flower-bordered paths lead to the front doors. Push open one of the several gates,— some one is certain to be unlocked, — or peer through the cracks of an old oaken fence which still affords some measure of the privacy dear to the heart of every Englishman, and you will see a bit of vanishing London which certainly can last but a short time longer. The roar of the city is quite unheard; one has simply passed out of the twentieth century into the seventeenth.

(1)

AN ACT

FOR THE

Preventing of the Multiplicity of

BUILDINGS

In and about the Suburbs of

LONDON,

AND

VVithin Ten Miles thereof.

Whereas the Great and Excessive Number of Houses, Edifices, Out-houses and Cottages erected and new built in and about the Suburbs of the City of London, and the parts thereunto adjoyning, is found to be very mischievous and inconvenient, and a great Annoyance and Nusance to the Commonwealth; And whereas notwithstanding divers Prohibitions heretofore had and made to the contrary, yet the said growing Evil is of late so much multiplied and increased, that there is a necessity of taking some further and speedy Course for the Redress thereof: And whereas by the Law the said Houses and Nusances ought to be abated, and the Builders, Occupiers, Continuers and Tenants thereof ought to make Fines for the same, so that if the Severity of the Law should be inflicted in such Cases, it would tend to the undoing of divers

AN ACT PASSED IN 1656 IN A FUTILE EFFORT TO PREVENT THE FURTHER GROWTH OF LONDON.

Those of us who, like the writer, when we visit London love to lose ourselves in the past, sometimes forget that London is "a going concern"—very much so. We who, on pleasure bent, spend a few weeks or months in this great city, may not sufficiently understand that

ST. PAUL'S CATHEDRAL, FROM THE BOTTOM OF LUDGATE HILL

After a colored etching by Luigi Kasimir

London is intensely modern as well as hoary with age. The six or eight millions of men and women who pass their lives there demand modern conveniences — and get them. Their postal and telegraph service is well-nigh perfect; their telephone system is not good, chiefly for the reason that the people, temperamentally very deliberate, are loath to interrupt a conversation, or whatever they may be doing, to answer the bell. Too often the telephone is regarded as a nuisance rather than as the greatest of modern conveniences.

Once fully understood, their system of transportation is the best in the world: whether by underground, by motor-bus, or taxi, one is rapidly conveyed over a wide area, with the minimum of inconvenience. To accomplish this, it has been necessary to spend immense sums; and if the various systems are generally in a semi-bankrupt condition, as with us, we do not hear of it.

During my lifetime, London has been practically rebuilt; the old inconvenient, if picturesque, buildings have been destroyed, and modern and commodious mansions, as they are called, have been erected in their stead. The main thoroughfares — the Strand, and Oxford Street, and Holborn — have been practically rebuilt, and Regent Street is rebuilding. The glorious view of St. Paul's from Fleet Street still remains; but thousands of old dilapidated rookeries, formerly the haunts of poverty and vice, and grimy with the dirt of centuries which knew nothing of sanitation, have given way to noble avenues like Kingsway and Aldwych. The exigencies of transportation have caused these great gashes to be made, and fine hotels and government buildings now line them on either side.

Holywell Street, characteristic of the London of the eighteen-eighties, once given over to second-hand bookshops, and others of a more questionable character, now exists only in memory — and in Pennell's drawing; and the Black Jack tavern, one of the haunts of the notorious Jack Sheppard, survives only in the pages of Harrison Ainsworth's novel. Once, almost forty years ago, I spent an hour in this Clare Market thieves' rendezvous, under the protection of my friend Hutt, whose bookshop was near by.

Oxford Street is to me one of the least interesting streets in London. It is a great modern thoroughfare, always crowded with people going east in the morning, and west in the evening when their day's work is done. I was walking along this street late one afternoon when my eye caught a sign, "Hanway Street," which instantly brought to mind the publishing business conducted in it more than a century ago by my lamented friend, William Godwin. I hoped to learn that it was named after the discoverer of the umbrella, but it is not. Hanway Street is a mean, narrow passage running north out of Oxford Street, as if intent upon going straightway to Hampstead; but it almost immediately begins to wobble and, finally changing its mind, turns east and stops at the Horse-Shoe Tavern in the Tottenham Court Road.

My hour of refreshment having come, I stopped there, too, and over a mug of ale I thought of Godwin,

HOLYWELL STREET

From a pen drawing by Joseph Pennell

and as a result of my meditations, decided to follow up the Godwin trail. And so, the inner man refreshed, I continued east through Holborn until I came to Snowhill, to which street Godwin subsequently removed his business and his interesting family. Turning off to the left, and doubling somewhat on my tracks, I descended Snowhill, and found myself facing a substantial modern building, which challenged attention by reason of the rather unusual decoration of its façade. It needed but a glance to see that this building had been erected on the site of the Saracen's Head Inn immortalized by Charles Dickens in "Nicholas Nickleby." Let into the wall were two large panels, one being a school scene bearing the legend "Dotheboy's Hall"; the other, a "Mail Coach leaving Saracen's Head." Over the arched doorway was a fine bust of Dickens; while to the left was a full-length figure of the immortal Mr. Squeers, and on the right a similar figure of Nicholas Nickleby. In the pleasure of my discovery I almost forgot all about Godwin, whose shop was once near-by; proving again, what needs no proof, that many characters in fiction are just as sure of immortality as persons who once moved among us in the flesh. Then I remembered that John Bunyan had lived and died in this street, when Snowhill was described as being very narrow, very steep, and very dangerous. This led me to decide that I would make a pilgrimage to Bunyan's tomb in Bunhill Fields, which I had not visited for many years.

And so, a few days later, I found myself wandering

about in that most depressing graveyard, in which thousands of men and women, famous in their time, found sepulture, in some cases merely temporary; for the records show that, after the passing of fifteen years or so, their graves were violated to make room for later generations, all traces of earlier interments having been erased. Poor Blake and his wife are among those whose graves can no longer be identified.

On the day of my visit it was much too damp to sit on the ground and tell sad stories of anything, but I had no difficulty in coming upon the tomb of Defoe, or that of Bunyan, a large altar-like affair, with his recumbent figure upon it. An old man, whom I met loitering about, called my attention to the fact that the nose had recently been broken off, and told me that it had been shot off by some soldier who had been quartered during the war in the near-by barracks of the Honorable Artillery Company. It appears that some miscreants had, to beguile the time, amused themselves by taking pot shots at the statuary, and that much damage had been done before they were discovered. I think I shall accuse the Canadians of this act of vandalism. It is always well to be specific in making charges of this kind; moreover, it will grieve my talented friend, Tait McKenzie, the sculptor, who comes to us from Scotland by way of Toronto, and who thinks it a more grievous crime to mutilate a statue than to damage a man.

It will have been seen from the foregoing that I am the gentlest of explorers. Give me the choice of roaming the streets of London in search of a scarce first

BUNHILL FIELDS BURYING GROUND

From a photograph taken for this publication. In this vast wilderness of stone, there is nothing to mark the grave of William Blake

edition of, say, "The Beggar's Opera,"—so delightfully performed month after month at the Lyric Theatre in Hammersmith, but which lasted scarcely a week in New York,— and a chance to explore some out-of-the

way place with an unpronounceable name, and my mind is made up in a moment. I have found the race with the sheriff sufficiently stimulating, and, on a holiday, give me the simple, or at least the contemplative, life.

Just before leaving home, I had lunched with my friend Fullerton Waldo; his face was positively beaming with happiness and his eyes sparkled. Why? Because he was going to Russia, to see for himself what the Bolsheviki were doing.

THE

B E G G A R's

O P E R A.

As it is Acted at the

THEATRE-ROYAL

I N

LINCOLNS-INNFIELDS.

Written by Mr. *G A Y.*

——*Nos hæc novimus esse nihil,*   Mart,

To which is Added,

The **MUSICK** *Engrav'd in* **COPPER-PLATES.**

L O N D O N.

Printed for JOHN WATTS, at the Printing-Office in *Wild-Court*, near *Lincoln's-Inn-Fields.*

MDCCXXVIII.

[Price 1s. 6d.]

"You will see plenty of misery you may be sure," I replied; "why look at it? Why not let the Russians stew in their own juice? Ultimately they will come home, those that are left, wagging their tales behind them."

But no, he wanted to see for himself. So we parted, each of us going his own way, and both happy.

But I did see one thing unusual enough to have interested even so sophisticated a traveler as Waldo, and that was the crowd which, on Armistice Day, that is to say, the eleventh of November, 1920, at exactly eleven o'clock in the morning, stood absolutely silent for two whole minutes. London is a busy city; there is a ceaseless ebb and flow of traffic, not in a few centres and here and there, as with us, but everywhere; and when this normal crowd is augmented by thousands from the country, intent upon seeing the dedication of the Cenotaph in the centre of Whitehall and the burial of the unknown warrior in the Abbey, it is a crowd of millions. And this huge crowd, at the first stroke of eleven, stood stock-still; not a thing moved, except perhaps here and there a horse turned its head, or a bird, wondering what had caused the great silence, fluttered down from Nelson's monument in Trafalgar Square. And so it was, we read, all over Britain, over Australia and Africa, and a part of Asia and America; the Great Empire, Ireland alone excepted, stood with bowed head in memory of the dead. Not a wheel turned anywhere, not a telegram or telephone message came over the wires. These English know how to stage big effects, as befits their Empire; with them history is ever and always in the making. And when at last the bunting fluttered down from the Cenotaph, and when the bones of the Unknown, with the King representing the nation as chief mourner, were deposited in the

Abbey, there formed a procession which, several days afterward, when I sought to join it, was still almost a mile long!

London can boast of countless little museums or memorials to this or that great man, and it is soon to have another — Wentworth Place in Hampstead, with which the name of Keats is so closely connected. When this is opened to the public,— I have visited it privately,— it is to be hoped that it will take on something of the kindly atmosphere of the Johnson House in Gough Square, rather than that of the cold museum dedicated to that old dyspeptic philosopher, Thomas Carlyle, in Chelsea. I remember well when he died. He was said to have been the Dr. Johnson of his time. Heaven keep us! Carlyle! who never had a good or kindly word to say of any man or thing; whose world, "mostly fools," bowed down before him and accepted his ravings as criticism; whose Prussian philosophy, "the strong thing is the right thing," was exploded in the Great War. I have lived to see his fame grow dimmer day by day, while Johnson's grows brighter as his wit, wisdom, and, above all, his humanity, become better known and understood.

To Gough Square then I hastened, once I was comfortably installed in my little flat, to see if any of the suggestions I had made at a dinner given by Cecil Harmsworth in the winter of 1914 to the Johnson Club, to which I was invited, had been carried out. The door was opened to my knock by an old lady, who invited me in as if I were an expected guest. She explained to me that it was hoped that ultimately one room would be dedicated to the memory of Boswell, and others of the Johnsonian circle, — Goldsmith, Garrick, Mrs. Thrale, Fanny Burney, and the rest, — and that the whole house would be pervaded by the immortal memory of Dr. Johnson, the kindest as well as the greatest of men; but that, owing to the war, not as much had been accomplished as had been hoped. "And so," I replied, "my suggestions have not been entirely forgotten. I was fearful that — " "Why," continued the old lady, " can you be Mr. Newton of Philadelphia?"

James Boswell
1763
I bought this for 2? at Greenwich when I was walking there with Mr. Samuel Johnson

A PRECIOUS SOUVENIR OF A FAMOUS FRIENDSHIP.
Inscription in a tiny book in Latin of the Psalms of David.

I could have hugged her, for, gentle reader, this is much nearer fame than I ever hoped for. What a morning it was! Mrs. Dyble called for her daughter, and I was presented, and again found to be not unknown; and believe me, these two women were so absolutely steeped in Johnson as to shame my small learning and make me wish for the support of real honest-to-God Johnsonians such as Tinker or Osgood, or my friend R. B. Adam of Buffalo, who has the greatest Johnson collection in the world, and who, when next he goes to London, has a treat in store which will cause him to forget, at least momentarily,

17 GOUGH SQUARE. DR. JOHNSON WROTE HIS FAMOUS
DICTIONARY IN THE ATTIC

his charming wife and his young son — charming
wives and young sons being not uncommon, whereas
Gough Square is unique.

Any man of fine heart and substantial means could
have bought the Gough Square house, but it required
a singularly wise and modest man to fit it up so
simply, so in keeping with the Johnsonian tradition;
to say, "We don't want a cold, dry-as-dust museum;
we want the house to be as nearly as possible what it
was when the great Doctor lived in it and compiled
the dictionary in its attic room." So it is, that 17
Gough Square, Fleet Street, is one of the places which
it is a delight to visit. A fine Johnsonian library has
been lent — and may ultimately be given — to the
house: paintings, portraits, rare prints, and autograph letters abound, and in these interesting surroundings, friends, literary societies, and clubs may
meet for the asking, and teas and dinners may be
sent in from the near-by Cheshire Cheese.

And all this might have been done, and yet the
house might have lacked one of its greatest charms,
namely, the kindly presence and hospitality of two
women, the discovery of whom, by Mr. Harmsworth,
was a piece of the rarest good fortune. Mrs. Dyble is
a soldier's wife, her husband being a color-sergeant
in one of the crack regiments; and the story goes
that, during the air-raids, when the Germans were
dropping bombs on all and sundry, the old lady went,
not into the "tubes" for shelter, but to meet the
bombs half-way, into the attic, and there, taking
down a copy of Boswell, she read quite composedly

through the night; for, as she said, she would not be worthy of her soldier husband if she were not prepared to face death at home as he was doing in France. But how long, I ask myself, will her daughter, Mrs. Rowell, a pretty widow, be content to live upon the memory of Dr. Johnson?

I was especially pleased to convey to the Johnson House a superb photograph of a portrait of Dr. Johnson by Reynolds, which had recently been acquired by Mr. John H. McFadden of Philadelphia. I was sitting in my club one afternoon, when Mr. McFadden came up and asked me how I would like to see a picture of Dr. Johnson, which he had just received from the Agnews in London. Of course I was delighted, and a few minutes later I was in the small but exquisite gallery of eighteenth-century portraits which Mr. McFadden has collected. Familiar as I am supposed to be with Johnson portraits, I had never seen the one which was shown me. It was obviously Dr. Johnson, and as soon as I returned home and had an opportunity of consulting my notes, I saw that it was the portrait painted for Dr. Taylor of Ashbourne. So far as I have been able to learn, it has never been engraved, or even photographed; and I told its owner that he owed it to himself and all Johnsonians to have it photographed in the best possible manner, and to send a copy to the Johnson House at Lichfield and also to Cecil Harmsworth. This Mr. McFadden readily consented to do; and so, on my arrival in London, I had the pleasant duty of presenting the pictures. The portrait is of a very old man; the head is bent

DR. JOHNSON'S AND JAMES BOSWELL'S VISIT TO FLORA MACDONALD.   A. E. N.

Anxious to help in the work there being carried on, I wrenched this picture from my own Johnson collection.

From a painting by Allan Ramsay, now in the Joh..son House, Gough Square

forward, the face is kindly, and about the mouth is the tremulousness of age. I take it, indeed, to be a speaking likeness, and it pleases me to fancy that the kindly Doctor has just made the remark quoted by Boswell, "As I grow older I am prepared to call a man a good man on easier terms than heretofore." [1]

During the war, when Germany was dropping bombs on London, and England was protesting that no real military purpose was served thereby and that the priceless treasures in the museums which had always been open to the public were being endangered, Germany characteristically replied that England should not keep her bric-à-brac in a fortress. Whether London is a fortress or not, I do not know; doubtless the Tower once was, and doubtless a certain amount of bric-à-brac is stored therein; but the Tower is a fatiguing place, and I fancy that I have visited it for the last time; whereas I shall never cease to delight in the London Museum, filled as it is with everything that illustrates the history, the social and business life of a people who by no accident or chance have played a leading part in the history of the world. This wonderful collection is housed in what was for years regarded as the most sumptuous private residence in London. It is situated in Stable Yard, very near St. James's Palace, and not so far from Buckingham

[1] Mr. McFadden, who died early in 1921, bequeathed his paintings, including the Johnson portrait, to the City of Philadelphia. Miss Lowell, when she saw this portrait, said, "It makes me understand the whole quality of Johnson's character better than anything else has ever done, and turns the usual portrait of him into a mere caricature. The wisdom, power, pathos, and sweetness in his face make one understand why his friends were so fond of him."

Palace as to prevent the late Queen Victoria from dropping in occasionally for a cup of tea with her friend, the Duchess of Sutherland, who for many years made it her residence. The story goes, that Her Majesty was accustomed to remark that she had left her house to visit her friend in her palace. Be this as it may, it is a magnificent structure, admirably fitted for its present purpose; and I was fortunate enough to be one of its first visitors when it was thrown open to the public in the spring of 1914. The arrangement of the exhibits leaves nothing to be desired; and if one does not find the garments of the present reigning family very stimulating, one can always retire to the basement and while away an hour or so among the panoramas of Tudor London, or fancy himself for a brief time a prisoner in Newgate.

But the streets of a great city are more interesting than any museum, and it was my custom generally to stroll through St. James's Park, gradually working my way toward Westminster, thence taking a bus to whatever part of London my somewhat desultory plans led me. One morning I had just climbed the steps that lead to Downing Street, when a heavy shower forced me to stand for a few moments under an archway, almost opposite number 10, which, as all the world knows, is the very unimposing residence of the Prime Minister. Standing under the same archway was an admirable specimen of the London policeman,— tall, erect, polite, intelligent, imperturbable,— and it occurred to me that the exchange of a "British-made" cigar for the man's views on the war would be no more than a fair exchange. And right here let me say that, all the time I was in England, I did not hear one word of complaint or one word of exultation. There was no doubt in Bobby's mind as to who won the war, "but, mind you, your fellows was most welcome, when they came"; and I thought I detected just a trifle of sarcasm in his last words. "We don't like the Germans, but we don't wear ourselves out 'ating 'em," he said, in reply to my question.

Just here our conversation was interrupted by an old lady, who came up to inquire at what hour Mrs. Lloyd George was going out.

"I'm not in her confidence, ma'am," replied my friend. Continuing, he suggested that he had gone to bed hungry many a. night but had n't minded in the least because he knew that British ships were taking the American army to France. "Hi've a tendency to get 'eavy hanyway," he continued. His views on the League of Nations were what one usually heard. He "had no confidence a man's neighbors would do more for a man than a man would do for himself"; that "Wilson was a bit 'eady, and the American people 'ad let 'im down something terrible."

Another morning, walking past the Horse Guards, I noticed, upon approaching the Mall, an enormous German cannon mounted on its heavy carriage, the wheels of which must have had at least five-inch tires. This engine of death, having shot its last bolt, was an object of the greatest interest to the children who constantly played about it. As I passed it, one little chap, probably not over four years of age, was kicking it forcibly with his little foot, his act being regarded approvingly the while by the Bobby who was looking on; but when finally he began to climb up on the wheel, from which he could have got a nasty fall, the policeman took the little lad in his arms, lifted him carefully to the ground, and bade him "be hoff," with the remark, "You'll be tearing that toy to pieces before you are a month older; then we won't 'ave nothing to remind us of the war."

"I shouldn't think you were likely to forget it," I said, looking at his decorations and handing him a cigar.

"Well, sir," he replied, thanking me and putting the cigar in his helmet, "it's curious how one thing drives another out of your mind: I was in it for three years and yet, except when I look at that gun, I can't rightly say I give it much thought."

I had an experience one day which I shall always remember, it was so unexpected and far-reaching. I was sitting in the back room of Sawyer's bookshop in Oxford Street, talking of London and, rather especially, of Mr. W. W. Jacobs's district thereof, in which I had recently made several interesting "short cruises," in company with his night watchman (he who had a bad shilling festooned from his watch-chain, it will be remembered), when I felt rather than saw that, while I was talking, a man had entered and seemed to be waiting, and rather impatiently, to get into the conversation. Now just how it came about,

I don't exactly know, but soon I found myself suggesting that Londoners know relatively little of their great city, and that it was only the enlightened stranger who really knew his way about.

"And this to me," said the stranger in a harsh, strident voice of such unusual timbre that its owner could have made a whisper heard in a rolling-mill. "Think of it," he continued, turning to Sawyer, "that I should live to be bearded in my den by a — by a — " He paused, not at a loss for a word, so much as turning over in his mind whether that word should be kindly or the reverse.

This gave me an opportunity of looking at the man who had entered, unasked, into the conversation, in very much the same way that I had entered into his London. He was seemingly about sixty years of age, short rather than tall, with piercing eyes under bushy eyebrows, but chiefly remarkable for his penetrating voice, which he used as an organ, modulating it or giving it, at will, immense power. One felt instinctively that he was no patrician, but rather a "city man" accustomed to giving orders and having them obeyed promptly, and having a degree of confidence in himself — say, rather, assurance — which one associates with Chicago rather than with London.

Now I am conceited enough to think that, with the ordinary mortal, I can hold my own in conversation when London is the subject; so almost before I knew it, I was trying to make myself heard by one who had evidently decided to take the lead in the conversation. The result was that two men were talking for victory at the same time, greatly to the amusement of Sawyer.

Finally my stranger-friend said, "Have you many books on London?"

To which I replied, relieved that the subject had taken a bookish turn, "Yes, about three hundred," which number is, say, a hundred and fifty more than I actually possess.

"I have over six thousand," said my friend; "I have every book of importance on London that ever has been written."

"Yes," said I, "and you have the advantage in discovering first how many books I had. If I had been as keen as mustard, as you are, I would have asked the question and you would have said three hundred; then I could have said six thousand."

"Listen to him," roared my friend, "he even doubts my word. Would you like to see my books?"

"Have you a copy of Stow?" I replied, to try him out.

"Yes," answered my friend, "every edition, including a presentation copy of the first edition of 1598, with an inscription to the Lord Mayor."

Now, presentation copies of the "Survay," properly regarded as the first book on London, are very rare. I had never seen one, and I replied that nothing would give me greater pleasure than to see his books; when and how could a meeting be arranged?

"Shall we say next Thursday afternoon?"

"Very good, but where?"

"Now," continued my friend, "pay attention. Tell your second chauffeur to get out your third Rolls-Royce car —"

"Never mind my chauffeurs and my Rolls-Royce cars," I interrupted; "if you are on the line of a penny bus, tell me how to reach you from Piccadilly Circus."

"Good," continued my friend; "you know the Ritz?"

"From the outside," I replied, "perfectly."

"Well, go to the Bobby who stands outside the Ritz, and ask him to tell you what bus to take to Clapham Junction, and when you get there, just ask any Bobby to direct you to John Burns's on the north side of Clapham Common."

John Burns! Had I heard aright? Was it possible that I was actually talking to John Burns, the great labor leader, who had once marched a small army of "Dockers" from the East End of London to Westminster, and who had finally become an all-powerful Member of Parliament, and Privy Councillor, and President of the Board of Trade and of the Local Government Board; John Burns, without whose approval not a statue, not a pillar-box or a fire-plug had been located for the past twenty years, and who had, when the war broke out, resigned all his offices of honor and emolument because he could not conscientiously go along with the government! As I recovered from my astonishment, John Burns, with a fine sense of dramatic values, had disappeared. I looked at his name and address written in his own

hand in my little engagement book. "Well," said I
to myself, "that looks like a perfectly good invita-
tion; John Burns will be expecting me about half-
past four, and I am not going to disappoint him."

A few days later, at the hour appointed, we descended from a taxi and found our friend awaiting
us at his front gate. Across the roadway stretched
Clapham Common, itself not without historic interest; but it was a cold raw day in late October, and
the inside of a city home is always more interesting
than the outside. As I removed my coat, I saw at a
glance that I had not been deceived in the number
of his books. There were books everywhere, about
fifteen thousand of them. All over the house were
open shelves from floor to ceiling, with here and
there a rare old cabinet packed with books, which
told the life-story of their owner. Books are for
reading, for reference, and for display. John Burns
had not stinted himself in any direction.

Throwing open the door of a good-sized room, in
which a fire (thank God!) was burning brightly,
Burns said briefly: "London, art and architecture
in this room; in the room beyond, political economy,
housing and social problems; rare books and first
editions in the drawing-room. Now come upstairs.
Here is biography and history." And then, throwing
open the door of a small room, he said, "This is my
work-shop; here are thousands and thousands of
pamphlets, carefully indexed." On landing at the
head of the stair, he said, "Newton, I've taken a
fancy to you and I'm going to let you handle, care-

fully, mind you, the greatest collection of Sir Thomas
More in the world — over six hundred items, twice
as many as there are in the British Museum. Here
they are, manuscripts, letters, first editions." Then,
dropping the arrogance of the collector who had made
his point, he took up a little copy of "Utopia," which
he had bought as a boy for sixpence, and said, "This
book has made me what I am; for me it is the greatest book in the world; it is the first book I ever
bought, it is the cornerstone of my library — the
foundation on which I have built my life. Now let
us have tea!"

During this pleasant function I plied my host with
question after question, and he, knowing that he was
not being interviewed, was frankness itself in his
replies. His judgment on the great men of England,
with whom he had worked for a lifetime, was shrewd,
penetrating, dispassionate — and, above all, kindly on
their conduct of the war. His reason for not going
along with the nation (he and Lord Morley were the
two conspicuous men in England who, on the out-
break of the war, retired into private life) was forceful, if to me unconvincing; and I quoted Blake's
axiom that a man who was unwilling to fight for the
truth might be forced to fight for a lie, without in
the least disturbing his equanimity. My remark
about Blake served to send the conversation in another direction, and we were soon discussing Blake's
wife, whose maiden name he knew, and his unknown
grave in Bunhill Fields, as if the cause and effect of
the Great War were questions that could be dis-

missed. Seeing a large signed photograph of Lord
Morley on the wall, and a copy of his "Life of Glad-
stone" and his own "Recollections" on the shelves,
I voiced my opinion that his friend was the author
of five of the dullest volumes ever written — an
opinion I would be glad to debate with all comers.

In reply to my question as to how he had accomplished so much reading, leading, as he has done for
so many years, the life of a busy public man, he answered: "I read quickly, have a good memory"
(there is no false modesty about John Burns), "and
I never play golf."

"Well, I am like you in one respect."

"What's that?" he asked; and then with a laugh,
"You don't play golf, I suppose."

What I thought was my time to score came when
he began to speak French, which I never understand
unless it is spoken with a strong English accent; this
gave me a chance to ask him whether he had not,
like Chaucer's nun, studied at Stratford-Atte-Bowe,
as evidently "the French of Paris" was to him "un-
knowe"; he laughed heartily, and instantly continued the quotation. But anyone who attempts to
heckle John Burns has his work cut out for him; a
man who has harangued mobs in the East End of
London and elsewhere, and held his own against all
comers in the House of Commons, and who has received honorary degrees for solid accomplishment
from half a dozen universities, is not likely to feel the
pin-pricks of an admirer. And when the time came
for us (for my wife was with me) to part, as it did all

too soon, it was with the understanding that we were
to meet again to do some walking and book-hunting
together; and anyone who has John Burns for a
guide in London, as I have had, is not likely soon to
forget the joys of the experience.

Holidays at last come to an end.

> If all the year were playing holidays,
> To sport would be as tedious as to work.

We came home, and our first impressions were those
of annoyance. As a nation, we have no manners;
one might have supposed that we, rather than the
English, had had our nervous systems exposed to the
shock of battle; that we, rather than they, had been
subject to air-raids and to the deprivations of war;
that we had become a debtor rather than a creditor
nation. We found rudeness and surliness everywhere. The man in the street had a "grouch," de-
spite the fact that he was getting more pay for less
work than any other man in the world, and that the
President had told him that he had an *inalienable*
right to strike. For the first time in my life I felt
that "labor would have to liquidate," to use a phrase
to which, in the past, I have greatly objected. No
question was civilly answered. The porter who
carried our bags took a substantial tip with a sneer,
and passed on. It may be that America is "the land
of the free and the home of the brave"; but we found
our cities dangerous, noisy, and hideously filthy. It
is not pleasant to say these things, but they are true.

THE END

INDEX

INDEX